THE AUSTRALIAN
Women's Weekly
one-pot dinners

acp
books

contents

The oven temperatures in this book are for conventional ovens; if you have a fan-forced oven, decrease the temperature by 10-20 degrees. A measurement conversion chart appears on the back flap of this book.

one-dish essentials

We all love a complete meal cooked in the one dish. It wasn't hard coming up with ideas for this cookbook and tasting time was a treat. Some of the recipes simply have all the ingredients layered or combined in the dish from the start of the cooking time, others have ingredients added at various stages of the cooking time – this is to avoid some ingredients being overcooked, and others undercooked. Just follow the recipes for a successful result every time.

Most of the recipes in this book are designed to serve a family of four, some are hearty family-style pasta bakes, others more special, in fact, special enough to impress even the most food-savvy friends or members of your family.

These dishes lend themselves to serving and sharing the food at the table, instead of serving the food on individual plates. Make sure you place the hot dish onto a heatproof surface on the table – a wooden board is ideal. If children are also at the table, make sure they're seated well away from the hot dish.

It's a good idea to serve a salad with one-dish dinners, they just seem to need it, even in the cooler months. It doesn't have to be a fancy salad, just salad leaves topped with a good dressing is fine. Serve bread, too, if you like, especially if the one-dish dinner is light on carbs.

If you're really organised, you can prepare at least some of the ingredients the morning or evening before the dish is to be cooked. We have a mixture of fast- and slow-cooked dinners in this book – make sure you read the recipe through first, to make sure that the cooking time fits into your schedule.

If you don't own a dish that is flameproof as well as ovenproof, our best advice is to buy one, maybe even two of different sizes and depths. You'll find some oven-baked recipes are better cooked in a shallow dish, usually to allow browning the top of the food. Some need the protection of high sides to prevent the food from drying out and/or browning too much. A lid is an asset when cooking one-dish dinners, though, not absolutely necessary, as two layers of foil usually do the job just as well. Once you've used

these multi-purpose dishes a couple of times, you'll wonder how you ever lived without them before.

The dish you choose must be compatible with your stove top and oven – induction stove tops are increasingly popular, but they do require a dish to have a particular type of surface; check before you buy them. Price is usually a good guide to the quality of these dishes, but remember, with care, these dishes should last for a lifetime of good cooking.

one pan

lemon fish with fennel and capers

4 baby fennel bulbs (520g)

2 tablespoons olive oil

1 medium lemon (140g)

4 x 180g (5½-ounce) skinless firm white fish fillets

275g (9 ounces) baby egg (plum) truss tomatoes

2 tablespoons rinsed, drained capers

¼ cup (60ml) dry white wine

30g (1 ounce) butter

1 Trim fennel, reserve fronds; cut fennel into wedges. Heat oil in large frying pan; cook fennel until browned lightly both sides.
2 Meanwhile, finely slice lemon. Add lemon to pan; cook until browned lightly and tender.
3 Season fish, add to pan, pushing fennel and lemon to side of pan; cook fish until browned lightly both sides.
4 Halve tomatoes lengthways. Add tomato, capers and wine to pan; bring to the boil. Dot fish with butter; sprinkle with about half the reserved fennel fronds. Reduce heat; cook, covered, about 5 minutes or until fish is cooked; season to taste.
5 Serve fish drizzled with pan juices; sprinkle with remaining fennel fronds.

prep + cook time 25 minutes
serves 4
nutritional count per serving
18.4g total fat (6.4g saturated fat);
1505kJ (360 cal);
5.2g carbohydrate;
37.9g protein; 4.2g fibre

tip We used blue-eye for this recipe but you can use any firm white fish fillets you like – coral trout or swordfish are suitable.

serving ideas Serve with a green salad.

Pancetta is an Italian unsmoked bacon prepared from pork belly, cured in salt and spices, then rolled into a sausage shape and dried for several weeks. Flavoured with sweet and savoury spices, such as black pepper, fennel and nutmeg, and with a rich layer of fat, when cooking with pancetta, a little goes a long way.

chicken with pancetta and white beans

4 chicken thigh cutlets, skin on (800g)

2 tablespoons fresh thyme leaves

1 tablespoon olive oil

8 brown pickling onions (320g)

2 cloves garlic

100g (3 ounces) thinly sliced pancetta

2 drained anchovy fillets

¼ cup (60ml) dry red wine

400g (12½ ounces) canned white beans, rinsed, drained

⅓ cup (25g) finely grated parmesan cheese

1 Using a small sharp knife, cut two 2.5cm (1-inch) slits into each chicken cutlet; fill slits with half the thyme. Season chicken.
2 Heat oil in large deep frying pan; cook chicken, skin-side down, about 5 minutes or until browned lightly.
3 Meanwhile, peel onions, leaving root ends intact; quarter onions. Turn chicken and add onion to pan; cook, covered, about 5 minutes or until onion is soft and browned lightly.
4 Meanwhile, peel and finely slice garlic, add to pan with pancetta, anchovies and remaining thyme; cook, stirring, until pancetta is crisp. Add wine and beans; bring to the boil. Reduce heat; simmer, uncovered, about 5 minutes or until chicken is cooked. Season to taste.
5 Serve sprinkled with cheese.

prep + cook time 35 minutes
serves 4
nutritional count per serving
30.4g total fat (9.9g saturated fat);
1860kJ (445 cal);
6.1g carbohydrate;
33.8g protein; 2.6g fibre

serving ideas Serve with a rocket (arugula) salad.

Saganaki, despite sounding vaguely Japanese, is a popular Greek dish, named after a sagani, the two-handled frying pan in which it is cooked and served. Traditionally made with grilled or fried cheese (fetta, kasseri, haloumi or kefalograviera) sprinkled with lemon juice and eaten with bread, saganaki has evolved to include meat, vegetables and/or seafood. Prawns saganaki is especially popular and features on many restaurant menus.

prawns saganaki

1kg (2 pounds) uncooked medium king prawns (shrimp)

400g (12½ ounces) spring onions

2 cloves garlic

1 medium lemon (140g)

2 tablespoons olive oil

½ cup (125ml) dry white wine

½ teaspoon caster (superfine) sugar

400g (12½ ounces) canned whole tomatoes

few drops Tabasco

½ cup coarsely chopped fresh flat-leaf parsley

⅓ cup each loosely packed fresh dill sprigs and mint leaves

180g (5½ ounces) fetta cheese

1 Shell and devein prawns, leaving tails intact.

2 Trim onions; cut into quarters. Peel and finely chop garlic. Finely grate lemon rind; segment lemon.

3 Heat oil in large frying pan; cook onion and garlic, stirring, until softened. Add prawns; cook, stirring, until prawns begin to change colour. Add wine, sugar, undrained tomatoes, Tabasco and half the herbs; bring to the boil. Reduce heat; simmer.

4 Place lemon segments and crumbled cheese on top of prawns, sprinkle with rind; cook, covered, about 3 minutes or until cheese begins to melt. Season to taste. Serve sprinkled with remaining herbs.

prep + cook time 40 minutes
serves 4
nutritional count per serving
20.9g total fat (8.3g saturated fat); 1672kJ (400 cal); 8.6g carbohydrate; 36.5g protein; 4.7g fibre

Gruyère is a hard-rind Swiss cheese with small holes and a nutty, slightly salty, flavour. It is a popular cheese for soufflés as it melts easily. Like a traditional soufflé, this soufflé omelette should be eaten straight away to prevent it sinking.

rocket, gruyère and ham soufflé omelette

1 medium brown onion (150g)

30g (1 ounce) butter

7 eggs

1 clove garlic

250g (8 ounces) rocket (arugula)

125g (4 ounces) gruyère cheese

½ cup coarsely chopped fresh chives

170g (5½ ounces) asparagus

150g (4½ ounces) sliced leg ham

2 teaspoons olive oil

1 tablespoon lemon juice

1 Peel and thinly slice onion. Melt butter in large deep frying pan; cook onion, stirring, until softened.

2 Meanwhile, separate eggs. Beat egg whites in medium bowl with electric mixer until soft peaks form. Add egg yolks and peeled crushed garlic; beat until combined.

3 Trim rocket; chop coarsely. Coarsely grate cheese. Fold half the rocket, half the chives and half the cheese into egg mixture. Pour mixture into pan; cook, uncovered, about 3 minutes or until omelette is almost set.

4 Meanwhile, trim asparagus; slice thinly on the diagonal. Slice ham thinly. Sprinkle asparagus and ham over omelette; cook until omelette starts to come away from side of the pan.

5 Meanwhile, preheat grill (broiler).

6 Sprinkle remaining cheese over omelette; grill until browned lightly.

7 Toss remaining rocket and chives in oil and lemon juice. Serve omelette topped with rocket salad.

prep + cook time 25 minutes
serves 4
nutritional count per serving
28.9g total fat (13.6g saturated fat); 1693kJ (405 cal); 4.7g carbohydrate; 31g protein; 2.3g fibre

italian-style lamb cutlets

2 large potatoes (600g)

2 tablespoons olive oil

1 fresh bay leaf

1 medium red onion (170g)

12 french-trimmed lamb cutlets (600g)

285g (9 ounces) bottled roasted red capsicums (bell peppers) in oil, drained

1/3 cup (50g) drained sun-dried tomatoes in oil

1/2 cup (90g) seeded green olives

2 tablespoons fresh oregano leaves

1/4 cup (60ml) beef stock

1 medium lemon (140g)

1 Wash unpeeled potatoes, then slice thinly. Heat oil in large frying pan; cook potato, with crushed bay leaf, turning, until potato is browned lightly.

2 Meanwhile, peel onion; cut into eight wedges. Add onion to pan; cook, covered, stirring occasionally, until onion softens and potato is tender.

3 Move potato mixture to centre of pan. Season lamb, place around outside edge of pan; cook until lamb is browned both sides.

4 Add capsicum, tomatoes, half the olives, oregano and stock to pan; bring to the boil. Reduce heat; simmer, covered, about 3 minutes or until lamb is cooked as desired. Season to taste.

5 Meanwhile, finely grate lemon rind; juice lemon. Serve lamb mixture sprinkled with rind, drizzled with juice, and topped with remaining olives.

prep + cook time 30 minutes
serves 4
nutritional count per serving
18.9g total fat (5.1g saturated fat); 1747kJ (418 cal); 34.1g carbohydrate; 23.9g protein; 6.4g fibre

tip We used desiree potatoes, which are red-skinned, moist-fleshed, multi-purpose potatoes. You could use red eye, pontiac or baby new potatoes.

serving ideas Serve with a green salad.

Chorizo is a popular Spanish sausage, made of coarsely ground pork and seasoned with garlic and chilli. Two types of chorizo are widely available today: cured and raw. The cured variety is deeply smoked so that it does not need cooking, whereas the raw variety must be cooked before eating.

mediterranean lentils and chorizo

3 stalks celery (450g)

1 medium brown onion (150g)

2 tablespoons olive oil

4 cured chorizo sausages (680g)

2 cloves garlic

¼ cup (60ml) dry sherry

2 tablespoons tomato paste

400g (12½ ounces) canned brown lentils

120g (4 ounces) baby spinach leaves

2 teaspoons coarsely chopped fresh marjoram

1 Trim celery; slice thickly on the diagonal. Peel onion; cut into eight wedges.

2 Heat oil in large frying pan; cook celery and onion, stirring, until onion softens.

3 Slice chorizo in half lengthways, then cut each half crossways into two pieces. Add chorizo to pan; cook until browned.

4 Meanwhile, peel and finely chop garlic. Add garlic, sherry and paste to pan; cook, stirring, until fragrant.

5 Rinse and drain lentils, add to pan with spinach and marjoram; cook, covered, until spinach wilts. Season to taste.

prep + cook time 25 minutes
serves 4
nutritional count per serving
56.8g total fat (18.6g saturated fat);
2855kJ (682 cal);
12.4g carbohydrate;
25.6g protein; 5.8g fibre

This recipe is the perfect way to use up the last of your smoked salmon, in fact, it is so delicious you may find yourself deliberately putting aside salmon just for this dish.

smoked salmon hash

1kg (2 pounds) kipfler (fingerling) potatoes

40g (1½ ounces) butter

1 tablespoon olive oil

1 small white onion (80g)

1 small green capsicum (bell pepper) (150g)

220g (7 ounces) sliced smoked salmon

12 quail eggs (150g)

2 tablespoons rinsed, drained capers

1 tablespoon white wine vinegar

2 teaspoons dijon mustard

2 teaspoons horseradish cream

¼ cup coarsely chopped fresh chives

1 Wash unpeeled potatoes; cut in half lengthways. Heat butter and oil in large frying pan; cook potato, covered, about 10 minutes, turning potato occasionally, until browned lightly and tender.
2 Meanwhile, peel and thinly slice onion. Add onion to pan; cook, stirring, until onion softens.
3 Finely chop capsicum. Top potato mixture with torn salmon slices; sprinkle with capsicum.
4 Crack eggs, one at a time, into a cup, then carefully slide over top of capsicum in pan.
5 Combine capers, vinegar, mustard and horseradish cream in small jug, pour over eggs; cook, uncovered, about 5 minutes or until eggs are set. Season to taste; serve sprinkled with chives.

prep + cook time 1 hour
serves 4
nutritional count per serving
20g total fat (8g saturated fat);
1834kJ (438 cal);
36.1g carbohydrate;
24.5g protein; 5.8g fibre

Thai eggplant, also known as apple eggplant (or makeau prau in Thai), is about the size of a golf ball and is either white or green in colour. The white eggplant is used in curries while the green eggplant, which is more crunchy, is used in salads.

pumpkin and eggplant with chilli and thai basil

200g (6½ ounces) thai eggplants

450g (14½ ounces) butternut pumpkin

6 baby eggplants (360g)

4 green onions (scallions)

5cm (2-inch) piece fresh ginger (25g)

2 fresh long red chillies

100g (3 ounces) snow peas

2 tablespoons peanut oil

440g (14 ounces) hokkien noodles

½ cup loosely packed fresh thai basil leaves

⅓ cup (120g) char siu sauce

¼ cup (80ml) vegetable stock

1 teaspoon sesame oil

1 Trim thai eggplants, cut into wedges. Peel and thinly slice pumpkin. Cut baby eggplants in half lengthways, then thinly slice diagonally. Trim onions, then cut into 5cm (2-inch) lengths. Peel ginger; finely slice ginger and the chilli. Trim snow peas.

2 Heat half the peanut oil in wok; stir-fry thai eggplant 2 minutes. Add pumpkin and remaining peanut oil; stir-fry until almost tender. Add baby eggplant, onion and chilli; stir-fry until vegetables are tender.

3 Add ginger, snow peas, noodles, ⅓ cup of the basil, sauce and stock to pan; stir-fry until hot. Season to taste.

4 Drizzle stir-fry with sesame oil; sprinkle with remaining basil to serve.

prep + cook time 35 minutes
serves 4
nutritional count per serving
14.2g total fat (2.3g saturated fat);
2244kJ (536 cal);
81g carbohydrate;
15.5g protein; 11.2g fibre

This rustic French stew is an eternal crowd-pleaser, perfect served with a warm crusty baguette. In this recipe we have used swordfish but you could use any white fish steaks or cutlets.

fish provençale

6 green onions (scallions)

1 clove garlic

¼ cup (60ml) olive oil

1½ tablespoons fresh rosemary leaves

1 tablespoon fresh lemon thyme leaves

4 x 180g (5½-ounce) swordfish steaks

500g (1 pound) mixed tomatoes

⅓ cup (80ml) dry white wine

⅓ cup (55g) seeded mixed olives

1 Trim onions; cut into thirds. Peel and thinly slice garlic.
2 Heat oil in deep large frying pan; cook onion and garlic, stirring, until onion softens.
3 Chop herbs. Season fish; add fish to pan with herbs. Cook fish about 2 minutes each side.
4 Meanwhile, chop tomatoes coarsely.
5 Add wine, tomato and olives to pan; cook, covered, about 5 minutes or until fish is cooked as desired. Season to taste.

prep + cook time 30 minutes
serves 4
nutritional count per serving
18.3g total fat (3.3g saturated fat);
1507kJ (360 cal);
3.8g carbohydrate;
38.7g protein; 2.5g fibre

serving idea Serve with steamed green beans.

Satay originated in Indonesia, and today features prominently in Indonesian, Malaysian, Thai, Vietnamese, Chinese and African cuisines. This satay recipe is quick and deceptively simple, requiring few ingredients and minimal preparation and cooking time.

quick chicken satay

1 large brown onion (200g)

650g (1¼ pounds) chicken thigh fillets

6cm (2½-inch) piece fresh ginger (30g)

2 fresh long red chillies

2 tablespoons peanut oil

¼ cup (65g) grated palm sugar

⅓ cup (95g) crunchy peanut butter

1 tablespoon japanese soy sauce

⅔ cup (160ml) coconut cream

500g (1pound) fresh thick rice noodles

½ cup (40g) bean sprouts

½ cup loosely packed fresh coriander (cilantro) leaves

1 Peel and quarter onion. Slice chicken thinly. Peel ginger. Slice ginger and chillies finely.

2 Heat oil in wok; stir-fry onion until soft. Add chicken, ginger and chilli; stir-fry until chicken is browned and almost cooked.

3 Add sugar to pan; cook, stirring, about 30 seconds or until lightly caramelised. Add peanut butter, sauce and coconut cream; cook, stirring, about 1 minute or until sauce thickens slightly. Add the noodles; stir-fry until hot. Add a little water if mixture is too thick.

4 Divide noodle mixture between serving bowls; serve topped with sprouts and coriander.

prep + cook time 20 minutes
serves 4
nutritional count per serving
43.1g total fat (14.7g saturated fat);
3143kJ (751cal);
50.1g carbohydrate;
39.6g protein; 5.2g fibre

tip This dish is quite spicy, you may want to use only one chilli, depending on your heat tolerance. Seeding the chilli also lessens the heat.

bakes

ricotta and capsicum bake

1 clove garlic

4 cups (1kg) firm ricotta cheese

2 cups (160g) finely grated
parmesan cheese

2 eggs

2 egg yolks

200g (6½ ounces) drained
roasted red capsicum
(bell pepper)

40g (1½ ounces) baby spinach
leaves

¾ cup loosely packed fresh
basil leaves

1 tablespoon olive oil

¼ cup (65g) basil pesto

2 tablespoons water

1 Preheat oven to 160°C/325°F.
Oil 22cm (9-inch) round springform
pan; line base and side with
baking paper.

2 Peel and crush garlic. Combine
cheeses, eggs, egg yolks and garlic
in medium bowl; season. Slice
capsicum thickly. Spread half the
cheese mixture over base of pan;
top with capsicum, spinach and
½ cup of the fresh basil. Spread
the remaining cheese mixture
over basil; drizzle with oil. Bake,
uncovered, about 1½ hours or
until browned lightly.

3 Stand bake 30 minutes.

4 Meanwhile, combine pesto
and the water in small bowl.
Serve bake drizzled with pesto
and sprinkled with remaining
basil leaves.

prep + cook time 2 hours
(+ standing) **serves** 6
nutritional count per serving
38.1g total fat (19.9g saturated fat);
2040kJ (488 cal);
3.8g carbohydrate;
32.7g protein; 1.1g fibre

tip This is delicious served warm
or cold, so is great for picnics or
a make-ahead lunch.

serving idea Serve with a
green salad.

This simple and delicious baked bean recipe is sure to become a firm family favourite. After trying these baked beans, the canned variety will pale in comparison.

herb-crumbed baked beans

1 medium brown onion (150g)

2 rindless bacon slices (130g)

¼ cup (60ml) olive oil

2 slices sourdough bread (140g)

½ cup (40g) finely grated parmesan cheese

¼ cup loosely packed fresh oregano leaves

2 cloves garlic

1.2kg (2.5lb) canned white beans

2 cups (520g) bottled tomato pasta sauce

1 tablespoon worcestershire sauce

¼ cup (60ml) pure maple syrup

2 teaspoons smoked paprika

1 Preheat oven to 220°C/425°F.
2 Peel onion; chop onion and bacon coarsely. Combine onion, bacon and 1 tablespoon of the oil in 2-litre (8-cup) ovenproof dish. Bake, uncovered, about 15 minutes or until onion is browned lightly.
3 Meanwhile, tear bread into coarse pieces; combine bread, cheese, oregano and remaining oil in medium bowl.
4 Peel and crush garlic. Rinse and drain beans. Stir beans, sauces, maple syrup, garlic and paprika into bacon mixture; season. Top with bread mixture. Bake, uncovered, about 10 minutes or until bread is browned.

prep + cook time 35 minutes
serves 4
nutritional count per serving
23.3g total fat (5.5g saturated fat);
2036kJ (487 cal);
45.4g carbohydrate;
20.9g protein; 9.4g fibre

serving idea Serve with a green leafy salad.

Havarti cheese is a soft, mild, cow's-milk cheese from Denmark; it is a good melting cheese, but you could replace it with mozzarella or a colby cheddar. Pale yellow in colour, it has small irregular holes throughout. When young, havarti has a mild, yet tangy, taste. As the cheese ages, its flavour intensifies and sharpens.

tuna potato bake

1.2kg (2½ pounds) potatoes

1 small brown onion (80g)

425g (13½ ounces) canned tuna in springwater

1 cup loosely packed fresh flat-leaf parsley leaves

2 cups (200g) coarsely grated havarti cheese

2 cloves garlic

1 cup (250ml) pouring cream

2 teaspoons finely grated lemon rind

1 Preheat oven to 200°C/400°F. Grease shallow 2-litre (8-cup) ovenproof dish.

2 Peel and thinly slice potatoes and onion. Layer about one-third of the potato in dish; top with half the drained, flaked tuna, half the onion and half the parsley. Sprinkle with ½ cup of the cheese. Repeat layering, finishing with potato; press down firmly. Cover dish with foil; bake 1 hour.

3 Peel and crush garlic. Combine cream, garlic and the rind in small bowl; season. Pour cream mixture over potato. Sprinkle with remaining cheese. Bake, uncovered, a further 30 minutes or until potato is tender and top is browned.

prep + cook time 1¾ hours
serves 6
nutritional count per serving
32.3g total fat (20.5g saturated fat);
2119kJ (506 cal);
23.2g carbohydrate;
29.1g protein; 3.4g fibre

serving ideas Serve with a green salad.

The delicious flavour combinations in this recipe ensures that it is not just a dish for vegetarians. The heat from the chillies, and the creamy ricotta perfectly complement the freshness of the zucchini.

spicy zucchini and ricotta pasta shells

3 medium zucchini (360g)

2 cloves garlic

1⅓ cups (320g) firm ricotta cheese

1 cup (80g) finely grated parmesan cheese

⅓ cup (50g) roasted pine nuts

3 egg yolks

1 tablespoon fresh lemon thyme leaves

½ teaspoon dried chilli flakes

5 cups (1.3kg) bottled tomato pasta sauce

250g (8 ounces) large pasta shells

½ cup loosely packed fresh small basil leaves

1 Preheat oven to 200°C/400°F. Oil shallow 2.5-litre (10-cup) ovenproof dish.
2 Coarsely grate zucchini. Peel and crush garlic. Combine zucchini, ricotta, ¾ cup of the parmesan, nuts, egg yolks, garlic, thyme and chilli in medium bowl; season.
3 Spread pasta sauce into dish; season. Spoon zucchini mixture into uncooked pasta shells; place in dish.
4 Cover dish with foil; bake 30 minutes. Uncover; bake about 15 minutes or until pasta is tender and cheese is browned lightly. Serve pasta sprinkled with basil and remaining parmesan.

prep + cook time 1 hour
serves 4
nutritional count per serving
34.7g total fat (12.3g saturated fat);
3122kJ (747 cal);
70.5g carbohydrate;
33.4g protein; 11.7g fibre

serving idea Serve with a green salad.

We have used pre-made potato gnocchi in this recipe. Gnocchi can be bought from supermarkets, either frozen or fresh.

meatball and gnocchi bake

4 thick pork sausages (480g)

1 tablespoon olive oil

¼ cup (30g) seeded black olives

500g (1 pound) potato gnocchi

2½ cups (650g) bottled tomato pasta sauce

1½ tablespoons coarsely chopped fresh oregano

1½ cups (150g) coarsely grated mozzarella cheese

1 Preheat oven to 200°C/400°F.
2 Chop sausages coarsely. Combine sausages and oil in shallow flameproof dish (19cm x 28cm) (7¾ inch x 11¼ inch). Bake, uncovered, about 20 minutes or until sausages are browned.
3 Meanwhile, halve olives. Add olives, gnocchi, sauce and oregano to dish; season. Sprinkle with cheese. Bake, uncovered, about 25 minutes or until gnocchi is tender.

prep + cook time 1 hour
serves 4
nutritional count per serving
43.3g total fat (17.4g saturated fat);
3127kJ (748 cal);
54.3g carbohydrate;
32.2g protein; 8.3g fibre

serving idea Serve with a green leafy salad.

With only five ingredients, all purchased easily from a supermarket, this sophisticated version of the classic bacon and egg pie is the perfect fuss-free midweek dinner.

prosciutto, spinach and egg pie

250g (8 ounces) frozen spinach

4 slices prosciutto (60g)

2 sheets puff pastry

1 tablespoon dijon mustard

12 eggs

1 Thaw spinach; drain well. Squeeze excess liquid from spinach. Chop spinach and prosciutto coarsely.

2 Preheat oven to 200°C/400°F. Oil deep 22cm (9-inch) square cake pan; line base and sides with baking paper, extending paper 5cm (2 inches) over sides.

3 Line base of pan with one pastry sheet, trimming to fit; spread with mustard. Top with prosciutto and spinach. Crack 11 of the eggs, one at a time, into a cup, then carefully slide on top of spinach mixture; season. Top pie with remaining pastry sheet, trimming to fit. Brush pastry with lightly beaten remaining egg.

4 Bake pie, uncovered, about 40 minutes or until browned lightly. Stand in pan 10 minutes before serving.

prep + cook time 50 minutes
serves 4
nutritional count per serving
36g total fat (6.6g saturated fat);
2395kJ (573 cal);
31.1g carbohydrate;
29.7g protein; 4.7g fibre

serving ideas Serve with a green salad; accompany with tomato relish or barbecue sauce.

Toad in the hole is a traditional English recipe, made using a Yorkshire pudding batter. This humble classic is given a contemporary twist with the addition of fresh herbs and zingy wholegrain mustard.

mustardy toad in the hole

2 medium red onions (340g)

16 lean beef chipolata sausages (480g)

6 sprigs fresh thyme

2 tablespoons olive oil

mustard batter

1 cup (150g) plain (all-purpose) flour

½ cup (75g) self-raising flour

3 eggs

1½ cups (375ml) milk

2 tablespoons wholegrain mustard

1 Preheat oven to 220°C/425°F.
2 Peel onions; cut into wedges. Combine onion, sausages, thyme and oil in shallow 2-litre (8-cup) ovenproof dish. Bake, uncovered, about 20 minutes or until sausages are browned, turning sausages halfway through cooking time.
3 Make mustard batter; pour batter over sausages. Bake, uncovered, about 30 minutes or until puffed and browned lightly.

mustard batter Whisk sifted flours, eggs, milk and mustard in medium bowl until batter is smooth; season.

prep + cook time 1¼ hours
serves 4
nutritional count per serving
48.1g total fat (19.7g saturated fat); 3210kJ (768 cal); 52.3g carbohydrate; 29.5g protein; 6.6g fibre

serving idea Serve with a green salad and tomato relish.

Mexican is a popular cuisine, especially with children. Cayenne pepper, however, is extremely hot so the amount used should be adjusted depending on whether you are cooking for adults or kids.

creamy chicken and corn burritos

310g (10 ounces) canned corn kernels

1 clove garlic

1¼ cups loosely packed fresh coriander (cilantro) leaves

3 cups (480g) shredded cooked chicken

2 cups (240g) coarsely grated cheddar cheese

1 cup (240g) light sour cream

½ teaspoon cayenne pepper

8 x 20cm (8-inch) flour tortillas

2 limes

1 Preheat oven to 220°C/425°F. Oil large ovenproof dish.
2 Rinse and drain corn. Peel and crush garlic. Coarsely chop ¼ cup of the coriander. Combine corn, chopped coriander, chicken, 1 cup of the cheese, sour cream, garlic and cayenne in medium bowl; season to taste.
3 To make burritos, divide chicken mixture onto centre of tortillas; roll tortillas to enclose filling, folding in sides. Place burritos in dish; sprinkle with remaining cheese. Bake, uncovered, about 25 minutes or until browned lightly.
4 Meanwhile, cut lime into wedges. Sprinkle burritos with remaining coriander; serve with lime wedges.

prep + cook time 35 minutes
serves 4
nutritional count per serving
46.6g total fat (24.3g saturated fat);
3532kJ (845 cal);
49g carbohydrate;
54.7g protein; 4.1g fibre

tips You can use 1 cup thawed frozen corn kernels instead of canned, if you prefer. It is fine to use shredded barbecued chicken in this recipe. A large (900g/1¾-pound) chicken should give 3 cups of shredded chicken meat.

serving idea Serve with a tomato and avocado salad.

lebanese lamb and potato bake

500g (1 pound) potatoes

2 tablespoons olive oil

1 teaspoon ground coriander

1 small brown onion (80g)

2 cloves garlic

800g (1½ pounds) minced (ground) lamb

½ teaspoon ground cinnamon

½ teaspoon ground allspice

½ cup (50g) packaged breadcrumbs

1 egg

½ cup (140g) onion marmalade

2 tablespoons raisins

2 tablespoons roasted pine nuts

1 Preheat oven to 200°C/400°F. Oil small baking dish; line base and sides with baking paper.

2 Peel and thinly slice potatoes. Combine potato, 1 tablespoon of the oil and coriander in dish; season. Bake, uncovered, 30 minutes.

3 Meanwhile, peel and finely chop onion. Peel and crush garlic. Combine onion, garlic, lamb, cinnamon, allspice, breadcrumbs and lightly beaten egg in medium bowl; season.

4 Spread lamb mixture over potato; drizzle with remaining oil. Bake, uncovered, about 20 minutes or until cooked through.

5 Spread onion marmalade over lamb; sprinkle with raisins and nuts.

prep + cook time 1¼ hours
serves 6
nutritional count per serving
21.7g total fat (6g saturated fat);
1736kJ (415 cal);
21.5g carbohydrate;
32.3g protein; 2.5g fibre

tip Onion marmalade, also called caramelised onion relish or onion jam, is available, in jars, from large supermarkets and delicatessens.

serving ideas Serve with a tomato, mint and red onion salad, and accompany with store-bought baba ghanoush, hummus or yogurt, if you like.

Radicchio originated in Italy and is a member of the chicory family. The leaves are dark burgundy in colour and have a strong bitter flavour; which makes radicchio a salad leaf you either love or hate.

radicchio and blue cheese baked risotto

1 medium brown onion (150g)

2 cloves garlic

1 tablespoon olive oil

2 teaspoons finely chopped fresh rosemary

2 cups (400g) arborio rice

½ cup (125ml) dry white wine

1.25 litres (5 cups) chicken stock

1 small radicchio (150g)

1 cup (80g) finely grated parmesan cheese

100g (3 ounces) blue cheese

¼ cup (25g) roasted walnuts

1 Preheat oven to 200°C/400°F.
2 Peel and finely chop onion. Peel and crush garlic. Heat oil in large shallow flameproof baking dish; cook onion, garlic and rosemary until onion softens.
3 Add rice; cook, stirring, 1 minute. Add wine; cook, stirring, 1 minute. Stir in stock. Cover dish with foil; bake about 40 minutes or until rice is tender.
4 Meanwhile, trim radicchio; slice thinly. Stir radicchio and parmesan into rice mixture; season to taste. Serve risotto topped with crumbled blue cheese and nuts.

prep + cook time 50 minutes
serves 4
nutritional count per serving
24.4g total fat (10.7g saturated fat);
2880kJ (689 cal);
86.3g carbohydrate;
24.8g protein; 2.6g fibre

tip We used gorgonzola cheese, but any blue cheese will work well in this dish.

serving ideas Serve with a green salad.

Ratatouille is a classic French dish, popular for its hearty flavour and attractive, rustic presentation. It is the perfect accompaniment not only for chicken but also for meat and fish. Make more than you need and freeze the extra in handy small batches that can be used as side dishes or added to pasta sauces.

baked chicken with ratatouille

1 small brown onion (80g)

1 medium red capsicum (bell pepper) (200g)

1 small eggplant (300g)

2 medium zucchini (240g)

250g (8 ounces) cherry tomatoes

4 cloves garlic

¼ cup fresh oregano sprigs

1 tablespoon red wine vinegar

¼ cup (60ml) olive oil

1 teaspoon caster (superfine) sugar

240g (7½ ounces) semi-soft goat's cheese

4 x 200g (6½-ounce) chicken breast fillets

½ cup loosely packed fresh small basil leaves

1 Preheat oven to 220°C/425°F.
2 Peel onion. Quarter capsicum; discard seeds and membranes. Coarsely chop onion, capsicum, unpeeled eggplant and zucchini; combine vegetables with tomatoes, peeled garlic, oregano, vinegar, 2 tablespoons of the oil and sugar in large baking dish. Cover dish with foil; bake 45 minutes.
3 Meanwhile, slice cheese thickly. Uncover dish; top with chicken and cheese, season. Drizzle with remaining oil. Bake, uncovered, about 15 minutes or until chicken is cooked.
4 Serve chicken sprinkled with basil leaves.

prep + cook time 1¼ hours
serves 4
nutritional count per serving
27g total fat (9.2g saturated fat);
2140kJ (512 cal);
9.1g carbohydrate;
55.6g protein; 5.3g fibre

one-dish roasts

sticky quince roasted lamb

2 cloves garlic

1.2kg (2½-pound) butterflied leg of lamb

2 teaspoons fennel seeds

2 teaspoons sweet paprika

¼ cup (60ml) red wine vinegar

¼ cup (60ml) olive oil

2 medium fennel bulbs (600g)

2 medium red onions (340g)

¼ cup (80g) quince paste

1 medium lemon (140g)

1 Peel and crush garlic. Combine lamb, spices, garlic, vinegar and 2 tablespoons of the oil in large bowl. Cover; refrigerate 15 minutes.
2 Preheat oven to 240°C/475°F.
3 Meanwhile, trim fennel; cut into thick wedges. Peel onions; cut into thick wedges. Combine fennel, onion and remaining oil in large baking dish. Top with lamb; season. Roast, uncovered, 20 minutes.
4 Meanwhile, warm quince paste. Remove dish from oven; brush lamb with quince paste. Roast, uncovered, about 20 minutes or until lamb is cooked as desired.
5 Remove lamb from dish. Cover, stand 15 minutes. Meanwhile, return vegetables to oven for about 15 minutes or until tender. Serve sliced lamb with vegetables and lemon wedges.

prep + cook time 1¼ hours (+ refrigeration) **serves** 4
nutritional count per serving
31.9g total fat (10.6g saturated fat); 2537kJ (607 cal); 15.6g carbohydrate; 68g protein; 4.3g fibre

tips Marinate lamb in a zip-top plastic bag to save washing up the bowl.
Quince paste can be warmed in a microwave-safe jug in a microwave oven or in a small saucepan over a low heat. It is available from delicatessens and some larger supermarkets.

serving ideas Serve with a green leafy salad.

roast chicken with gremolata

2kg (4-pound) whole chicken

¼ cup loosely packed fresh oregano leaves

1 tablespoon olive oil

6 medium egg (plum) tomatoes (450g)

1 clove garlic

1 tablespoon finely shredded lemon rind

½ cup coarsely chopped fresh flat-leaf parsley

1 Preheat oven to 220°C/425°F.

2 Wash chicken under cold water; pat dry inside and out with absorbent paper. Using kitchen scissors, cut along both sides of backbone; discard backbone. Place chicken on bench, breast-side up; press down on breastbone with heel of hand to flatten.

3 Place chicken in large baking dish; rub chicken all over with combined oregano and oil, season. Roast, uncovered, about 1 hour, or until chicken is cooked. Remove from dish, cover; stand while tomatoes cook.

4 Meanwhile, halve tomatoes, add to dish, season; roast, uncovered, 15 minutes.

5 Meanwhile, to make gremolata, peel and crush garlic. Combine rind with parsley and garlic in small bowl. Sprinkle tomatoes with gremolata; serve with chicken.

prep + cook time 1½ hours
serves 4
nutritional count per serving
50.1g total fat (15.1g saturated fat);
22904kJ (694 cal);
1.5g carbohydrate;
59.3g protein; 1.4g fibre

tips Use a zester to shred the lemon rind finely.
Ask the butcher to butterfly the chicken for you.

serving ideas Serve with a green salad.

Although not common, fresh horseradish can be found in some greengrocers and Asian food shops. Prepared horseradish and horseradish cream are widely available in supermarkets. These cannot be substituted one for the other in cooking, but both can be used as table condiments. Here we have used horseradish cream, which is a commercially prepared creamy paste consisting of grated horseradish, vinegar, oil and sugar.

roasted snapper with potato wedges and horseradish mayo

400g (12½ ounces) potatoes

6 cloves garlic

2 tablespoons olive oil

1 medium lemon (140g)

2 whole baby snapper (600g)

⅓ cup loosely packed fresh dill sprigs

2 teaspoons rinsed, drained capers

¼ cup (75g) mayonnaise

2 teaspoons horseradish cream

1 Preheat oven to 240°C/475°F.
2 Wash unpeeled potatoes; cut into wedges. Combine potato, unpeeled garlic and 1 tablespoon of the oil in large baking dish; season. Roast, uncovered, 20 minutes.
3 Meanwhile, thinly slice lemon. Fill fish cavities with lemon and ¼ cup of the dill; season. Place fish on top of potato; drizzle with remaining oil. Roast, uncovered, about 25 minutes or until fish and potato are cooked through.
4 Meanwhile, finely chop remaining dill. Finely chop capers. Combine dill and capers with mayonnaise and horseradish cream in small bowl.
5 Serve fish with potato, and horseradish mayonnaise.

prep + cook time 50 minutes
serves 2
nutritional count per serving
33.8g total fat (5.3g saturated fat); 2562kJ (613 cal); 35.6g carbohydrate; 38.2g protein; 6.4g fibre

serving ideas Serve with a green salad.

cider roasted pork belly

1.5kg (3-pound) piece pork belly, rind on

2 tablespoons finely chopped fresh rosemary

1 tablespoon sea salt flakes

1⅓ cups (330ml) apple cider

4 medium parsnips (1kg)

4 cloves garlic

1½ cups (375ml) salt-reduced chicken or vegetable stock

2 medium green-skinned apples (300g)

800g (1½ pound) canned brown lentils

1 Preheat oven to 240°C/475°F.

2 Using sharp knife, score pork rind in criss-cross pattern. Place pork, rind-side up, in large baking dish. Combine rosemary and salt in small bowl; rub salt mixture over pork. Roast pork, uncovered, about 20 minutes or until the rind starts to blister and crackle.

3 Reduce oven temperature to 160°C/325°F. Add cider to dish; roast, uncovered, 1¼ hours.

4 Meanwhile, peel and quarter parsnips. Peel garlic. Add parsnips, garlic and stock to dish; roast, uncovered, 45 minutes.

5 Quarter unpeeled apples. Rinse and drain lentils. Add apple and lentils to dish; roast, uncovered, about 30 minutes or until apple is tender. Season mixture to taste.

prep + cook time 3¾ hours
serves 4
nutritional count per serving
57.8g total fat (19.5g saturated fat);
4065kJ (972 cal);
46.1g carbohydrate;
57.6g protein; 10.3g fibre

tip To get crispy crackling, the pork rind needs to be really dry: leave the pork rind uncovered in the fridge overnight; cover the pork flesh with plastic wrap to stop it drying out.

serving idea Serve with a green leafy salad.

Prosciutto is an unsmoked thinly-sliced Italian ham. It is air-cured and comes in two varieties: prosciutto crudo (raw) and prosciutto cotto (cooked). Here we have used prosciutto crudo.

sage and prosciutto veal with cannellini beans

800g (1½ pounds) canned cannellini beans

1 medium lemon (140g)

½ cup (125ml) chicken stock

4 veal cutlets (500g)

6 sprigs fresh sage

4 slices prosciutto crudo (60g)

2 tablespoons olive oil

1 tablespoon balsamic vinegar

1 Preheat oven to 240°C/425°F.

2 Rinse and drain beans. Cut lemon into wedges. Combine beans, lemon and stock in large baking dish. Top each cutlet with one sprig sage; wrap cutlets with prosciutto.

3 Add cutlets to dish; drizzle with oil, season. Roast, uncovered, about 20 minutes or until veal is cooked as desired. Serve drizzled with vinegar, top with remaining sage leaves.

prep + cook time 30 minutes
serves 4
nutritional count per serving
13.6g total fat (3.1g saturated fat); 1447kJ (346 cal); 17.3g carbohydrate; 35.7g protein; 8.7g fibre

serving idea Serve with a green leafy salad.

Small chickens (500g) make a wonderful substitute for the chicken breast supremes used in this recipe. Allow one chicken per person and cook for roughly double the time.

basil and lemon roast chicken

3 medium leeks (1kg)

1 tablespoon olive oil

1 clove garlic

60g (2 ounces) butter, softened

2 teaspoons finely grated lemon rind

2 tablespoons coarsely chopped fresh basil

4 x 220g (7-ounce) chicken breast supremes

1 Preheat oven to 240°C/475°F.
2 Trim leeks; cut into quarters lengthways. Combine leek and oil in large baking dish; season. Cover dish with foil; roast 15 minutes.
3 Meanwhile, peel and crush garlic. Combine butter, rind, basil and garlic in small bowl. Using fingers, make a pocket between the chicken breasts and skin; push butter mixture under skin. Season.
4 Place chicken on top of leeks; roast, uncovered, about 20 minutes or until chicken is cooked; spoon pan juices over chicken after 10 minutes.

prep + cook time 45 minutes
serves 4
nutritional count per serving
35.2g total fat (14.1g saturated fat);
2087kJ (499 cal);
6.4g carbohydrate;
37.7g protein; 4.9g fibre

tip Chicken breast supremes have their skin intact. They are single boneless breasts with the wing bone attached.

serving idea Serve with a tomato salad and crusty bread.

Harissa is a North African paste made from dried red chillies, garlic, olive oil and caraway seeds. Extremely versatile, it can be used as a rub for meat, an ingredient in sauces and dressings, or served as a condiment. It is available from Middle-Eastern food shops and some supermarkets.

harissa lamb and vegetables

3 medium red capsicums
(bell peppers) (600g)

3 medium zucchini (360g)

1 clove garlic

2 tablespoons olive oil

2 lamb backstraps (400g)

2 teaspoons harissa paste

4 small pitta breads (340g)

1 medium lemon (140g)

1 cup (280g) tzatziki

1 Preheat oven to 240°C/475°F.
2 Quarter capsicums; discard seeds and membranes. Coarsely chop capsicum and unpeeled zucchini. Peel and crush garlic. Combine capsicum, zucchini, garlic and 1 tablespoon of the oil in baking dish; season. Roast, uncovered, 15 minutes.
3 Meanwhile, combine lamb, harissa and remaining oil in medium bowl. Add lamb to dish; roast, uncovered, about 10 minutes or until lamb is cooked as desired. Cover lamb; stand 5 minutes.
4 Wrap bread in foil; warm in oven 5 minutes. Cut lemon into wedges.
5 Slice lamb thinly; serve with vegetables, bread, tzatziki and lemon wedges.

prep + cook time 40 minutes
serves 4
nutritional count per serving
28g total fat (8.5g saturated fat);
2618kJ (626 cal);
53.1g carbohydrate;
37g protein; 7.6g fibre

tips Marinate the lamb in a zip-top plastic bag to save washing up the bowl. Sometimes lamb backstrap may be sold as lamb fillet. Tzatziki is a mint and cucumber yogurt dip that is available in the refrigerated section in most large supermarkets and delis.

Garam Masala originated in Northern India and refers to a blend of specific spices. It is based on varying proportions of cardamom, cinnamon, cloves, coriander, fennel and cumin, roasted and ground together. Black pepper and chilli can be added for a hotter version.

indian-spiced lamb rack

800g (1½ pounds) baby carrots

2 tablespoons olive oil

4cm (1½-inch) piece fresh ginger (20g)

1 tablespoon ground cumin

2 teaspoons garam masala

1 teaspoon ground turmeric

1 tablespoon lemon juice

1 x 8-cutlet french-trimmed lamb rack (360g)

½ cup (160g) mango chutney

1 cup (280g) yogurt

1 Preheat oven to 220°C/425°F.
2 Trim and peel carrots. Combine carrots and half the oil in large baking dish; season.
3 Combine remaining oil, peeled and grated ginger, spices and juice in small bowl; spread mixture all over lamb. Add lamb to dish; roast, uncovered, about 35 minutes or until lamb is cooked as desired. Cover; stand 5 minutes.
4 Serve lamb with chutney and yogurt.

prep + cook time 1 hour
serves 4
nutritional count per serving
15g total fat (4.3g saturated fat);
1287kJ (308 cal);
23.3g carbohydrate;
16.3g protein; 5.9g fibre

tip You can use four thickly sliced medium carrots instead of the baby carrots.

serving ideas Serve with a cucumber salad and naan (flat) bread.

This is a delicious and budget-friendly family meal; substitute lamb or chicken sausages to suit your family's tastes.

rosemary roasted sausages and tomatoes

1 medium bulb garlic (70g)

8 thick beef sausages (1.2kg)

2 tablespoons olive oil

4 sprigs fresh rosemary

3 slices sourdough bread (210g)

250g (8 ounces) cherry tomatoes

2 tablespoons red wine vinegar

1 cup loosely packed fresh basil leaves

1 Preheat oven to 220°C/425°F.
2 Cut garlic bulb in half horizontally. Combine garlic, sausages, half the oil and rosemary in large baking dish. Roast, uncovered, about 15 minutes or until sausages are browned.
3 Tear bread into coarse pieces; add bread to dish with tomatoes, drizzle with remaining oil. Roast, uncovered, about 15 minutes or until bread is crisp and sausages are cooked.
4 Squeeze half the garlic into a small bowl, mash with a fork; stir in vinegar. Drizzle over dish; sprinkle with basil.

prep + cook time 50 minutes
serves 4
nutritional count per serving
87.2g total fat (38.2g saturated fat);
4590kJ (1098 cal);
32.9g carbohydrate;
40.7g protein; 14g fibre

serving idea Serve with a green leafy salad.

Kipflers are small, finger-shaped potatoes that are great both baked and in salads. We used kipfler potatoes because of their nutty flavour and small size, but you could use any good all-round or roasting potato such as desiree or sebago.

garlic roasted potatoes and mushrooms

800g (1½ pounds) kipfler (fingerling) potatoes

2 tablespoons olive oil

4 portobello mushrooms (200g)

2 cloves garlic

80g (2½ ounces) butter, softened

2 tablespoons finely chopped fresh flat-leaf parsley

1 fresh long red chilli

1 medium lemon (140g)

130g (4 ounces) buffalo mozzarella

¼ cup fresh mint leaves

1 Preheat oven to 220°C/425°F.
2 Wash unpeeled potatoes; cut in half lengthways. Combine potato and 1 tablespoon of the oil in large baking dish; season. Roast, uncovered, 30 minutes. Add mushrooms to dish, top-sides down.
3 Peel and crush garlic. Combine butter, garlic and parsley in a small bowl; divide mixture into mushrooms, drizzle with remaining oil. Roast, uncovered, about 15 minutes or until vegetables are tender.
4 Meanwhile, slice chilli thinly. Cut lemon into wedges.
5 Tear cheese into coarse pieces; add to dish. Sprinkle with chilli and mint. Serve with lemon.

prep + cook time 55 minutes
serves 4
nutritional count per serving
31g total fat (15.4g saturated fat);
1897kJ (453 cal);
28g carbohydrate;
12.7g protein; 5.9g fibre

tip We used mozzarella made from buffalo milk.

one pot

lemon grass prawn and pea curry

1 tablespoon vegetable oil

2 cups (500ml) chicken stock

1 cup (250ml) coconut milk

1 tablespoon fish sauce

2 tablespoons light brown sugar

2 tablespoons lime juice

800g (1½ pounds) uncooked medium tiger prawns (shrimp)

1 cup (120g) frozen peas

1 lime

lemon grass curry paste

10cm (2-inch) stick fresh lemon grass (20g)

6cm (2½-inch) piece fresh ginger (30g)

1 fresh small thai green (serrano) chilli

2 shallots (50g)

2 cloves garlic

1 bunch fresh coriander (cilantro) (100g), with roots attached

2 tablespoons water

1 Make lemon grass curry paste.
2 Heat oil in large saucepan; cook curry paste, stirring, until fragrant. Add stock, coconut milk, sauce, sugar and juice; simmer, uncovered, 5 minutes.
3 Meanwhile, shell and devein prawns leaving tails intact. Add prawns and peas to pan; simmer, uncovered, about 3 minutes or until prawns change colour. Season to taste.
4 Cut lime into wedges. Sprinkle curry with reserved coriander leaves; serve with lime.

lemon grass curry paste Trim lemon grass; chop coarsely. Peel ginger; slice thickly. Chop chilli coarsely. Peel and coarsely chop shallots and garlic. Wash coriander roots and stems; chop roots and stems coarsely (you need 2 tablespoons). Pick ¼ cup of coriander leaves; reserve remaining leaves (to sprinkle over curry). Blend or process lemon grass, ginger, chilli, shallot, garlic, coriander root and stem mixture, coriander leaves and the water until smooth.

prep + cook time 45 minutes
serves 4
nutritional count per serving
19g total fat (12.3g saturated fat);
1392kJ (333 cal);
12.9g carbohydrate;
25.9g protein; 4.2g fibre

tips You could make the curry paste in a mortar and pestle. Buy shelled uncooked prawns to save preparation time.

serving idea This is the perfect recipe to serve with pre-cooked microwave ready-to-heat rice.

This recipe is also delicious with lamb or beef meatballs, just be sure to allow a little extra cooking time.

minestrone with rosemary chicken meatballs

1 medium brown onion (150g)

2 medium carrots (240g)

3 stalks celery (450g)

3 cloves garlic

1 tablespoon olive oil

1 tablespoon finely chopped fresh rosemary

800g (1½ pounds) canned diced tomatoes

1 litre (4 cups) chicken stock

1 tablespoon caster (superfine) sugar

½ cup (40g) finely grated parmesan cheese

1 cup loosely packed fresh basil leaves

rosemary chicken meatballs

1 clove garlic

500g (1 pound) minced (ground) chicken

1 tablespoon finely chopped fresh rosemary

1 Peel and coarsely chop onion and carrots. Trim and coarsely chop celery. Peel and crush garlic. Heat oil in large saucepan; cook onion, carrot, celery, garlic and rosemary, stirring, until vegetables have softened.

2 Add undrained tomatoes, stock and sugar; bring to the boil.

3 Meanwhile, make rosemary chicken meatballs.

4 Add meatballs to pan; simmer, covered, about 15 minutes or until meatballs are cooked through. Season to taste. Serve sprinkled with cheese and basil.

rosemary chicken meatballs
Peel and crush garlic. Combine chicken, rosemary and garlic in medium bowl; season. Roll level tablespoons of mixture into balls.

prep + cook time 40 minutes
serves 4
nutritional count per serving
19.6g total fat (6.2g saturated fat);
1664kJ (398 cal);
18.9g carbohydrate;
33.8g protein; 6.3g fibre

Using a cut of chicken on the bone adds a certain juiciness and depth of flavour that cannot be achieved without the bone.

tomato, pancetta and olive chicken

1 tablespoon olive oil

8 chicken thigh cutlets (1.6kg)

1 large brown onion (200g)

6 slices pancetta (90g)

4 cloves garlic

1 cup loosely packed fresh oregano leaves

½ cup (125ml) dry white wine

250g (8 ounces) cherry tomatoes

1 cup (250ml) chicken stock

1 cup (120g) seeded green olives

1 teaspoon caster (superfine) sugar

1 Heat oil in large saucepan; cook chicken, in batches, until browned. Remove from pan.

2 Meanwhile, peel onion; cut into wedges. Chop pancetta coarsely. Peel and crush garlic. Cook onion, pancetta, garlic and half the oregano in pan, stirring, until onion softens. Add wine; cook, stirring, 1 minute.

3 Return chicken to pan with tomatoes, stock, olives and sugar; bring to the boil. Reduce heat; simmer, covered, about 30 minutes or until chicken is cooked. Serve sprinkled with remaining oregano.

prep + cook time 1 hour
serves 4
nutritional count per serving
48.4g total fat (15.1g saturated fat);
3036kJ (726 cal);
12.8g carbohydrate;
53.5g protein; 3.3g fibre

tips You can use any similar-sized chicken pieces, such as drumsticks or a whole chicken, cut into pieces.
The pancetta, stock and olives are already quite salty, so you should not need to add extra salt to this dish.

serving idea Serve with a green leafy salad.

Artichokes hearts are marinated in either oil or brine, sometimes with a variety of herbs and spices. They can be purchased in cans, jars or loose from the delicatessen. All these varieties of artichoke hearts are suitable for this recipe.

chicken and artichoke pot roast

1.2kg (2½-pound) whole chicken

8 brown pickling onions (320g)

600g (1¼ pounds) baby new potatoes

2 tablespoons olive oil

6 cloves garlic

8 sprigs fresh thyme

1 cup (250ml) dry white wine

8 drained marinated artichoke hearts (100g)

1 cup (250ml) chicken stock

1 Rinse chicken under cold water; pat dry inside and out with absorbent paper. Tuck wing tips under chicken; tie legs together with kitchen string.

2 Peel onions, leaving root ends intact; halve onions and unpeeled potatoes.

3 Heat oil in large saucepan; cook onion, potato, unpeeled garlic and thyme, stirring occasionally, until browned. Remove from pan.

4 Cook chicken in same pan until browned all over. Add wine; boil, uncovered, 1 minute.

5 Meanwhile, halve artichokes. Return vegetables to pan with artichokes and stock; bring to the boil. Reduce heat; simmer, covered, about 1½ hours or until chicken is cooked. Season to taste.

prep + cook time 2 hours
serves 4
nutritional count per serving
33.9g total fat (9g saturated fat); 2516kJ (602 cal); 25.5g carbohydrate; 36.2g protein; 5.5g fibre

serving idea Serve with a green leafy salad.

The combination of chicken and seafood in this recipe makes it reminiscent of the eternally-popular Spanish one-dish classic – paella. This recipe is slightly simpler but just as delicious.

chicken and seafood tomato rice

600g (1¼ pounds) chicken thigh fillets

500g (1 pound) uncooked medium king prawns (shrimp)

2 tablespoons olive oil

1 medium brown onion (150g)

3 cloves garlic

½ teaspoon dried chilli flakes

1 teaspoon smoked paprika

1½ cups (300g) white medium-grain rice

800g (1½ pounds) canned diced tomatoes

2½ cups (625ml) chicken stock

500g (1 pound) baby clams

1 medium lemon (140g)

¼ cup coarsely chopped fresh flat-leaf parsley

1 Chop chicken coarsely. Shell and devein prawns, leaving tails intact. Heat oil in large saucepan; cook chicken and prawns until almost cooked through. Remove from pan.

2 Meanwhile, peel and finely chop onion. Cook onion in pan, stirring, until softened.

3 Peel and thinly slice garlic; add to pan with chilli and paprika. Cook, stirring, until fragrant. Add rice, undrained tomatoes and stock; bring to the boil. Reduce heat; simmer, covered, 25 minutes.

4 Return chicken and prawns to pan with clams; simmer, covered, about 10 minutes or until rice is tender and clams open. Season to taste.

5 Meanwhile, cut lemon into wedges. Sprinkle rice with parsley; serve with lemon.

prep + cook time 1 hour
serves 6
nutritional count per serving
14.6g total fat (3.4g saturated fat);
2002kJ (479 cal);
46.6g carbohydrate;
38.3g protein; 2.6g fibre

tip Some clams might not open after cooking. These might need prompting with a knife or might not have cooked as quickly as the others – you do not have to discard these, just open with a knife and cook a little more if you wish.

serving idea Serve with a green leafy salad.

We used pork mince here, but you could substitute veal or beef mince, or even a combination of all three. Combinations of mince are available at certain butchers.

cheesy chilli bolognese

1 medium brown onion (150g)

3 cloves garlic

1 tablespoon olive oil

500g (1 pound) minced (ground) pork

2 tablespoons fresh thyme leaves

½ teaspoon dried chilli flakes

3 cups (780g) bottled tomato pasta sauce

1 tablespoon caster (superfine) sugar

3 cups (750ml) hot water

400g (12½ ounces) penne pasta

2 cups (240g) coarsely grated cheddar cheese

¼ cup coarsely chopped fresh flat-leaf parsley

1 Peel and coarsely chop onion. Peel and crush garlic. Heat oil in large saucepan; cook onion, garlic, pork, thyme and chilli, stirring, until pork is browned.

2 Stir in sauce and sugar; simmer, uncovered, 2 minutes. Add the water and uncooked pasta; cook, covered, about 20 minutes, stirring occasionally, until pasta is tender.

3 Stir in 1½ cups of the cheese; season to taste. Serve pasta sprinkled with parsley and remaining cheese.

prep + cook time 50 minutes
serves 4
nutritional count per serving
37.9g total fat (17.2g saturated fat);
3917kJ (937 cal);
89.6g carbohydrate;
55.3g protein; 8.6g fibre

chilli beef with cornbread dumplings

1 medium brown onion (150g)

3 cloves garlic

1 tablespoon olive oil

800g (1½ pounds) minced (ground) beef

2 teaspoons each ground cumin and smoked paprika

½ teaspoon cayenne pepper

400g (12½ ounces) canned kidney beans

800g (1½ pounds) canned diced tomatoes

1 cup (250ml) beef stock

1 cup (250ml) water

1 tablespoon light brown sugar

cornbread dumplings

1⅓ cups (200g) self-raising flour

⅓ cup (55g) polenta

¼ cup (30g) coarsely grated cheddar cheese

¼ cup (60g) creamed corn

1 egg

½ cup (125ml) milk

1 Peel and coarsely chop onion. Peel and crush garlic. Heat oil in large saucepan; cook onion, beef, garlic and spices, stirring, until beef is browned.

2 Rinse and drain beans, add to pan with undrained tomatoes, stock, the water and sugar; bring to the boil. Reduce heat; simmer, uncovered, 30 minutes, stirring occasionally. Season to taste.

3 Meanwhile, make cornbread dumplings.

4 Roll level tablespoons of the dumpling mixture into balls and place on top of chilli. Cook, covered, about 15 minutes or until dumplings are cooked.

cornbread dumplings Combine sifted flour, polenta and cheese in medium bowl; stir in corn, lightly beaten egg and milk.

prep + cook time 1¼ hours
serves 4
nutritional count per serving
26.6g total fat (11.2g saturated fat); 3047kJ (729 cal); 70.8g carbohydrate; 58.2g protein; 10.5g fibre

tips Use wet hands when rolling the dumplings to stop them sticking. Use a wide saucepan so you have more surface area for the dumplings to cook.

Marsala is an Italian fortified wine recognisable by its intense amber colour and complex aroma. It is used in Italian cooking, however, you can substitute madeira, port or dry sherry.

pork, mushroom and marsala stew

1kg (2 pounds) boneless pork shoulder

¼ cup (35g) plain (all-purpose) flour

2 tablespoons olive oil

4 shallots (100g)

2 cloves garlic

300g (9½ ounces) swiss brown mushrooms

1 tablespoon coarsely chopped fresh rosemary

1 cup (250ml) marsala

1 cup (250ml) chicken stock

1 cup (250ml) water

1 tablespoon tomato paste

½ cup coarsely chopped fresh flat-leaf parsley

1 Chop pork coarsely. Coat pork in flour; shake off excess. Heat oil in large saucepan or flameproof dish; cook pork, in batches, until browned. Remove from pan.
2 Peel and thinly slice shallots and garlic. Halve mushrooms. Cook shallot, garlic, mushrooms and rosemary in pan, stirring occasionally, until mushrooms are browned. Add marsala; cook, stirring, 30 seconds.
3 Return pork to the pan with stock, the water and paste; bring to the boil. Reduce heat; simmer, covered, about 1¾ hours, stirring occasionally, or until pork is tender. Season to taste.
4 Serve sprinkled with parsley.

prep + cook time 2¼ hours
serves 4
nutritional count per serving
19.3g total fat (4.9g saturated fat);
2299kJ (550 cal);
17g carbohydrate;
58.4g protein; 3.3g fibre

tip You can use pork neck or another stewing cut of pork for this dish.

Oregano is a herb with a woody stalk and tiny, dark-green leaves. It has a pungent, peppery flavour that is delicious in stews, casseroles and roasts.

oregano lamb stew with gnocchi

1kg (2 pounds) boneless lamb shoulder

2 tablespoons olive oil

2 medium brown onions (300g)

2 cloves garlic

2 teaspoons dried oregano

½ teaspoon ground cinnamon

400g (12½ ounces) canned diced tomatoes

3 cups (750ml) beef stock

1 tablespoon tomato paste

2 teaspoons caster (superfine) sugar

500g (1 pound) potato gnocchi

½ cup (40g) finely grated parmesan cheese

1 cup loosely packed fresh oregano leaves

1 Chop lamb coarsely. Heat oil in large saucepan; cook lamb, in batches, until browned. Remove from pan.

2 Meanwhile, peel and thickly slice onions. Cook onion in pan, stirring, until softened. Peel and thinly slice garlic, add to pan with dried oregano and cinnamon. Cook, stirring, until fragrant.

3 Return lamb to pan with undrained tomatoes, stock, paste and sugar; bring to the boil. Reduce heat; simmer, covered, 2 hours, stirring occasionally.

4 Uncover; bring to the boil. Boil, uncovered, 10 minutes. Stir in gnocchi; cook, uncovered, about 5 minutes or until gnocchi is tender and sauce is thickened. Season to taste.

5 Serve stew sprinkled with cheese and fresh oregano.

prep + cook time 2¾ hours
serves 6
nutritional count per serving
19g total fat (7.2g saturated fat); 1998kJ (478 cal); 31.8g carbohydrate; 42.4g protein; 3.9g fibre

tip We used 'fresh' pre-made potato gnocchi available from the refrigerated section of most supermarkets.

serving idea Serve with a green leafy salad.

Dhal is a thick stew made from pulses (lentils, peas or beans). It is a staple of Indian, Pakistani, Nepali, Sri Lankan and Bangladeshi cuisines. It is a ready source of protein and, when eaten with vegetables, it is a healthy and nutritionally balanced meal.

cauliflower dhal

1 medium brown onion (150g)

8cm (3¼-inch) piece fresh ginger (40g)

2 cloves garlic

1 small cauliflower (1kg)

1 tablespoon vegetable oil

1½ tablespoons each ground cumin and ground coriander

1½ cups (300g) dried red lentils

1 litre (4 cups) vegetable stock

400g (12½ ounces) canned diced tomatoes

1 cup loosely packed fresh coriander (cilantro) leaves

½ cup (160g) mango chutney

1 cup (280g) yogurt

1 Peel and finely chop onion. Peel then grate ginger. Peel and crush garlic. Cut cauliflower into florets. Heat oil in large saucepan; cook onion, ginger and garlic, stirring, until onion softens. Add cauliflower and spices; cook, stirring, until fragrant.

2 Add lentils, stock and undrained tomatoes to pan; bring to the boil. Reduce heat; simmer, uncovered, about 20 minutes, stirring occasionally, or until lentils are tender.

3 Serve sprinkled with coriander. Serve with chutney, yogurt and naan (flat) bread, if you like.

prep + cook time 35 minutes
serves 4
nutritional count per serving
9.5g total fat (2.3g saturated fat);
1956kJ (468 cal);
55g carbohydrate;
32.7g protein; 17.6g fibre

Pilaf is a cooked rice dish whose origins lie in the Middle East. It has always been popular in Central and Southern Asia, East Africa, Latin America and the Caribbean. A variety of meats and vegetables can be included in a pilaf depending on local cuisines and tastes, and the availability of ingredients.

spiced lamb pilaf

1½ cups (300g) basmati rice

1 medium brown onion (150g)

2 cloves garlic

4cm (1½-inch) piece fresh ginger (20g)

3 lamb leg steaks (450g)

1 tablespoon olive oil

2 dried bay leaves

2 teaspoons ground coriander

½ teaspoon ground cinnamon

½ cup (75g) coarsely chopped dried apricots

2¼ cups (560ml) chicken stock

¼ cup (35g) roasted unsalted shelled pistachios

½ cup loosely packed fresh mint leaves

1 cup (280g) yogurt

1 Cover rice in medium bowl with about 4 cups cold water; stand 30 minutes, drain well.
2 Meanwhile, peel and thinly slice onion and garlic. Peel and grate ginger. Slice lamb thinly.
3 Heat oil in large saucepan; cook lamb, in batches, until browned. Remove from pan.
4 Cook onion in pan, stirring, until softened. Add garlic, ginger, bay leaves and spices; cook, stirring, until fragrant. Stir in rice. Add apricots and stock; bring to the boil. Reduce heat; cook, covered, over low heat, about 20 minutes or until rice is tender.
5 Meanwhile, chop nuts coarsely. Stir lamb into pilaf; season to taste. Sprinkle with nuts and mint; serve with yogurt.

prep + cook time 40 minutes (+ standing) **serves** 4
nutritional count per serving
17.9g total fat (4.7g saturated fat); 2663kJ (637 cal); 77.2g carbohydrate; 38.7g protein; 4.5g fibre

casseroles

beef and shiitake mushroom pie

900g (1¾ pounds) beef brisket

30g (1 ounce) butter

¼ cup (35g) plain (all-purpose) flour

¼ cup (60ml) light soy sauce

½ cup (125ml) mirin

½ cup (125ml) sake

1 cup (250ml) water

100g (3 ounces) oyster mushrooms

100g (3 ounces) fresh shiitake mushrooms

1 sheet puff pastry

1 egg

½ teaspoon each black and white sesame seeds

1 Preheat oven to 160°C/325°F.
2 Chop beef coarsely. Melt butter, on stove top, in shallow 22cm (9-inch) flameproof dish; cook beef, in batches, stirring, until browned. Return beef to dish; sprinkle with flour; stir to combine. Gradually stir in sauce, mirin, sake and the water until smooth. Cook, covered, in oven, about 2 hours or until beef is tender.
3 Chop mushrooms coarsely.
4 Increase oven temperature to 180°C/350°F.
5 Stir mushrooms into dish; season. Cover dish with pastry; brush pastry with lightly beaten egg, sprinkle with seeds. Cook, in oven, about 15 minutes or until pastry is browned.

prep + cook time 2¾ hours
serves 4
nutritional count per serving
47.5g total fat (18.7g saturated fat);
3641kJ (871 cal);
23.8g carbohydrate;
72.5g protein; 2.7g fibre

A ragù is a rich, thick sauce with a velvety texture and complex flavour. It is usually cooked for a long time. Ragù alla bolognese freezes beautifully and can be used in lasagne or cannelloni, or served with tagliatelle or linguine pasta.

ragù alla bolognese

250g (8 ounces) sliced hot pancetta

800g (1½ pounds) beef chuck steak

20g (¾ ounce) butter

¾ cup (180ml) dry red wine

1 small brown onion (80g)

1 medium carrot (120g)

1 stalk celery (150g)

10g (½ ounce) dried porcini mushrooms

10 fresh sage leaves (10g)

⅓ cup (95g) tomato paste

3 cups (750ml) beef stock

⅓ cup (25g) finely grated parmesan cheese

2 teaspoons finely grated lemon rind

1 Preheat oven to 150°C/300°F.
2 Finely chop pancetta; cook in heated large flameproof dish, stirring, until browned lightly.
3 Meanwhile, chop beef coarsely. Add beef to dish with butter; cook, stirring, until beef is browned. Add wine; cook, uncovered, 5 minutes.
4 Meanwhile, peel onion and carrot; trim celery. Finely chop onion, celery and carrot, add to dish with mushrooms and sage; cook, stirring, 5 minutes. Add paste; cook, stirring, 5 minutes. Add stock; cook, covered, in oven, 4 hours. Uncover dish; return to oven, cook 30 minutes.
5 Skim and discard excess fat from surface. Season to taste. Using two forks, shred meat coarsely. Serve bolognese sprinkled with cheese and rind.

prep + cook time 5 hours
serves 4
nutritional count per serving
24.3g total fat (11.2g saturated fat);
2182kJ (522 cal);
7.4g carbohydrate;
59.5g protein; 2.9g fibre

Beef ribs are a mainstay of Korean cooking. Short ribs are available from Asian butchers but may need to be ordered in advance if purchasing from your local butcher shop.

korean beef short ribs

4cm (1½-inch) piece fresh ginger (20g)

1 green onion (scallion)

2 cloves garlic

2 tablespoons korean chilli paste

1 fresh bay leaf

⅓ cup (80ml) light soy sauce

¼ cup (55g) firmly packed light brown sugar

½ cup (125ml) beef stock

1kg (2 pounds) beef short ribs

5 fresh small red thai (serrano) chillies

2 cups (500ml) water

1 medium carrot (120g)

½ small wombok (napa cabbage) (350g)

1 teaspoon toasted sesame seeds

1 Preheat oven to 150°C/300°F.
2 Peel and grate ginger. Trim onion; cut into 10cm (4-inch) lengths. Peel and crush garlic. Combine ginger, onion, garlic, paste, bay leaf, sauce, sugar, stock, beef and chillies in large casserole dish; cook, covered, in oven, 1 hour. Stir in the water; cook, covered, 2 hours.
3 Meanwhile, peel and thinly slice carrot. Add carrot to dish; cook, covered, 20 minutes. Season to taste.
4 Finely shred wombok; divide between four bowls. Top with beef mixture; serve sprinkled with seeds.

prep + cook time 3¾ hours
serves 4
nutritional count per serving
15.5g total fat (6.4g saturated fat); 1610kJ (385 cal); 18.8g carbohydrate; 41.3g protein; 3.2g fibre

tip Korean chilli paste, otherwise known as gochujang, is available from Asian supermarkets; you can use sambal oeleck instead, if you prefer.

red bean pork and rice

1kg (2-pound) piece boneless pork belly

4cm (1½-inch) piece fresh ginger (20g)

2 cloves garlic

2 green onions (scallion)

2 teaspoons caster (superfine) sugar

¼ cup (60ml) chinese cooking wine

2 tablespoons sweetened red bean paste

2 tablespoons light soy sauce

1 star anise

½ teaspoon ground cardamom

2½ cups (625ml) water

1 cup (200g) white long-grain rice

1½ cups (375ml) water, extra

1 green onion (scallion), extra

4 frozen chinese steamed rice buns

1 Preheat oven to 150°C/300°F.
2 Remove rind from pork, trim excess fat; chop pork coarsely. Heat large flameproof dish on stove top; cook pork, in batches, until browned; remove from dish.
3 Peel and grate ginger. Peel and crush garlic. Coarsely chop onions. Discard all but about 2 tablespoons of fat from dish. Add sugar to dish; cook, stirring, over low heat, until browned. Return pork to dish with ginger, chopped onion, wine, paste, sauce, garlic, star anise, cardamom and the water. Cover dish; cook, in oven, 3 hours.
4 Meanwhile, rinse rice in sieve under cold water until water runs clear; drain well. Remove dish from oven; stir in rice and the extra water. Cook, covered, in oven, about 18 minutes or until rice is tender. Season to taste.
5 Meanwhile, slice extra onion thinly. Steam or microwave buns according to directions on packet. Serve pork and rice with sliced onion and buns.

prep + cook time 3½ hours
serves 4
nutritional count per serving
66.2g total fat (23.9g saturated fat);
4834kJ (1155 cal);
74.6g carbohydrate;
60.9g protein; 4.3g fibre

tip Frozen steamed rice buns are available in the freezer section of Asian supermarkets and most large supermarkets.

Use any left-over ingredients from this dish to make a delicious pizza topping. Spread the sauce over a store-bought pizza base, top with sliced bocconcini and coarsely chopped prosciutto if there's some left. Cook in a hot oven until the base is crisp, then top with sage leaves before serving.

veal and bocconcini stacks

240g (7½ ounces) bocconcini cheese

4 x 100g (3-ounce) veal schnitzels

12 fresh sage leaves

4 slices prosciutto (60g)

2 cups (520g) bottled tomato pasta sauce

½ cup (40g) finely grated parmesan cheese

1 Preheat oven to 200°C/400°F.
2 Thinly slice bocconcini. Place two pieces of veal in an oiled medium shallow ovenproof dish; top each with 3 sage leaves, 1 slice prosciutto, 2 slices bocconcini and another piece of veal. Repeat layering; you will have two stacks.
3 Pour sauce over veal stacks; sprinkle with parmesan. Cover dish with foil; cook, 20 minutes. Uncover; cook about 5 minutes or until browned lightly.

prep + cook time 40 minutes
serves 2
nutritional count per serving
35.4g total fat (18.4g saturated fat);
3057kJ (731 cal);
19.9g carbohydrate;
80.8g protein; 5.7g fibre

tips Veal schnitzel is thinly sliced steak available crumbed or plain (uncrumbed). In this recipe we used plain schnitzel; they are also known as escalopes.
We used a bottled cherry tomato arrabbiata pasta sauce – it has a chilli kick to it – but you can use any tomato pasta sauce you like.

Use a casserole dish big enough to fit one layer of the tightly-packed osso buco, as they will shrink during cooking. Buy pieces of uniform size and thickness and stand them up in the dish to ensure that each person receives a portion of the rich bone marrow that is found in the veal shin.

italian veal casserole

1 tablespoon olive oil

4 thick pieces veal osso buco (1.2kg)

¾ cup (90g) seeded green olives

1 medium lemon (140g)

2 cups (520g) bottled tomato pasta sauce

2 cups (500ml) water

4 drained anchovy fillets

½ cup (120g) firm ricotta cheese

½ cup (40g) finely grated parmesan cheese

½ cup coarsely chopped fresh flat-leaf parsley

1 Preheat oven to 160°C/325°F.
2 Heat oil in large flameproof dish on stove top; cook veal until browned.
3 Meanwhile, chop olives coarsely. Quarter lemon. Add olives, lemon, sauce, and the water to dish; season. Cook, covered, in oven, 2 hours.
4 Increase oven temperature to 200°C/400°F.
5 Chop anchovies coarsely. Stir anchovy into veal mixture; top with ricotta, sprinkle with parmesan. Cook, uncovered, in oven, about 15 minutes or until cheese is browned. Serve sprinkled with parsley.

prep + cook time 2½ hours
serves 4
nutritional count per serving
16.5g total fat (5.9g saturated fat);
1788kJ (427 cal);
15.7g carbohydrate;
52g protein; 3.5g fibre

tip It's a good idea to gently press a piece of baking paper, cut to fit inside the dish, onto the surface of the food before it goes into the oven. This will stop the food from browning too much. Cover the dish itself with a lid or foil.

Preserved lemon rind is an indispensable ingredient in Moroccan cooking. Lemon pieces are packed in a salt and lemon juice or water mixture and left until the rind becomes soft and pulpy. To use, remove and discard the pulp, squeeze the juice from the rind, then rinse the rind well. Slice or chop, according to the recipe.

moroccan lamb shanks

1 tablespoon olive oil

4 french-trimmed lamb shanks (800g)

1 small brown onion (80g)

1 teaspoon each ras el hanout, ground ginger and cinnamon

½ teaspoon each ground cumin and white pepper

pinch saffron threads

400g (12½ ounces) canned chopped tomatoes

1½ cups (375ml) vegetable stock

2 tablespoons dried currants

2 tablespoons roasted slivered almonds

¼ cup (50g) finely chopped preserved lemon rind

185g (6 ounces) persian fetta cheese

¼ cup loosely packed fresh coriander (cilantro) leaves

1 Preheat oven to 150°C/300°F.
2 Heat oil in large flameproof dish on stove top; cook lamb until browned all over. Remove from dish.
3 Meanwhile, peel and finely chop onion. Cook onion in dish, stirring, until softened. Add spices; cook, stirring, until fragrant. Return lamb to dish with undrained tomatoes, stock and currants; bring to the boil. Cover dish; cook, in oven, about 2½ hours or until lamb is almost falling off the bone.
4 Skim and discard excess fat from surface of sauce. Divide lamb between plates. Stir nuts and preserved lemon rind into sauce; season to taste. Spoon sauce over lamb; sprinkle with drained crumbled cheese and coriander.

prep + cook time 4 hours
serves 4
nutritional count per serving
25.4g total fat (10.9g saturated fat);
1731kJ (414 cal);
9.9g carbohydrate;
34.9g protein; 3.7g fibre

tip Persian fetta is a soft, creamy fetta marinated in a blend of olive oil, garlic, herbs and spices. It is available from most delicatessens and larger supermarkets.

Saffron is a popular spice in Spanish cooking. It is harvested from the stigma of a flower belonging to the crocus family and, although the quality can vary, the best saffron is the most expensive spice in the world as it must be harvested by hand. It is available ground or in strands and, when infused, imparts a yellow-orange colour and distinct flavour to food.

spanish chicken casserole

800g (1½ pounds) chicken thigh fillets

1 tablespoon olive oil

½ cup (125ml) dry white wine

2 cloves garlic

2 cups (500ml) chicken stock

2 teaspoons lemon juice

3 sprigs fresh thyme

pinch saffron threads

4 small potatoes (480g)

1 large brown onion (200g)

2 medium tomatoes (300g)

1 tablespoon pine nuts

1 tablespoon slivered almonds

1 Preheat oven to 200°C/400°F.

2 Coarsely chop chicken. Heat oil in large deep flameproof dish on the stove top; cook chicken until browned. Add wine; bring to the boil. Boil, uncovered, 1 minute, scraping residue from bottom of pan.

3 Peel and crush garlic. Stir in stock, juice, garlic, thyme and saffron into dish. Reduce heat; simmer, uncovered, 3 minutes.

4 Meanwhile, peel potatoes and onion; quarter potatoes, onion and tomatoes, add to dish. Cover; cook, in oven, about 40 minutes or until chicken is cooked and vegetables are tender. Remove dish from oven; season to taste. Sprinkle with nuts; return to oven, cook, uncovered, about 5 minutes or until nuts are browned lightly.

prep + cook time 1 hour
serves 4
nutritional count per serving
23.9g total fat (5.6g saturated fat);
2052kJ (490 cal);
18.3g carbohydrate;
43.6g protein; 3.8g fibre

braised beef in chinese ginger broth

1kg (2 pounds) beef brisket

30g (1 ounce) fresh shiitake mushrooms

30g (1 ounce) oyster mushrooms

30g (1 ounce) enokii mushrooms

1 tablespoon light soy sauce

¼ teaspoon sesame oil

3cm (1¼-inch) piece fresh ginger (15g)

ginger broth

1 bunch coriander (cilantro) (100g) with roots attached

10cm (4-inch) piece fresh ginger (50g)

1 stalk celery (150g)

1 medium carrot (120g)

1 large red onion (300g)

3 cloves garlic

5 green onions (scallions)

3.5 litres (14 cups) water

1 Make ginger broth.
2 Preheat oven to 140°C/285°F.
3 Add beef to broth; cook, covered, in oven, 6 hours.
4 Remove beef from broth; cover to keep warm. Slice mushrooms, add to broth; simmer, uncovered, about 5 minutes or until the mushrooms are tender. Stir in sauce and oil.
5 Meanwhile, peel and grate ginger. Slice beef thinly; divide beef between bowls. Ladle broth into bowls. Serve topped with ginger; sprinkle over reserved coriander leaves.

ginger broth Wash coriander; chop roots and stems coarsely, reserve leaves (to sprinkle over broth before serving). Peel and thinly slice ginger. Trim celery. Peel carrot, red onion and garlic. Coarsely chop celery, carrot, garlic and red and green onions. Combine ingredients (except coriander leaves) in large deep flameproof dish; bring to the boil. Reduce heat; simmer, uncovered, 1 hour. Using slotted spoon, discard solids.

prep + cook time 7¼ hours
serves 4
nutritional count per serving
15.5g total fat (6.3g saturated fat); 1722kJ (412 cal); 8.7g carbohydrate; 56.6g protein; 5.1g fibre

tip The ginger broth can be made ahead and kept, covered, for several days in the refrigerator, or freeze for up to six months.

You can use any firm white fish fillets you like. Blue-eye, bream, flathead, swordfish, whiting, jewfish, sea perch or ling are all good choices. Check for any small pieces of bone in the fillets and use tweezers to remove them.

oven-baked herbed snapper

1 medium red onion (170g)

1 large red capsicum
(bell pepper) (350g)

1 medium lemon (140g)

250g (8 ounces) cherry tomatoes

⅓ cup (50g) seeded kalamata olives

½ cup (125ml) dry white wine

¼ cup (60ml) olive oil

¾ cup loosely packed fresh oregano leaves

½ cup loosely packed fresh mint leaves

4 x 200g (6½-ounce) skinless snapper fillets

¼ cup (40g) pine nuts

1 Preheat oven to 220°C/425°F.
2 Peel and coarsely chop onion. Quarter capsicum; discard seeds and membranes. Chop capsicum coarsely. Thinly peel rind from lemon; remove any white pith. Juice lemon.
3 Combine onion, capsicum, rind, juice, tomatoes, olives, wine, oil and half the herbs in large shallow baking dish; season. Top with fish. Cook, covered, 15 minutes.
4 Add nuts to dish; cook, uncovered, about 10 minutes or until fish is cooked. Sprinkle with remaining herbs.

prep + cook time 45 minutes
serves 4
nutritional count per serving
24.4g total fat (3.6g saturated fat);
1981kJ (474 cal);
11.1g carbohydrate;
44.8g protein; 4.3g fibre

pistachio, pancetta and fig-stuffed lamb

2 slices pancetta (30g)

2 dried figs (30g)

⅓ cup (45g) roasted unsalted shelled pistachios

⅓ cup (25g) japanese breadcrumbs

2 tablespoons olive oil

1.5kg (3-pound) boneless lamb forequarter

1 large red capsicum (bell pepper) (350g)

1 large tomato (220g)

1 medium lemon (140g)

400g (12½ ounces) canned crushed tomatoes

¼ cup loosely packed fresh oregano leaves

1 tablespoon olive oil, extra

1 teaspoon dried oregano

250g (8 ounces) haloumi cheese

1 cup (280g) greek-style yogurt

½ cup finely chopped fresh mint

1 Preheat oven to 180°C/350°F.
2 Chop pancetta, figs and nuts finely; combine with breadcrumbs and oil in small bowl, season.
3 Open lamb out on board, skin-side down. Top with pancetta mixture. Roll lamb to enclose filling; tie with kitchen string at 2cm (¾-inch) intervals to secure.
4 Quarter capsicum; discard seeds and membranes. Chop capsicum, tomato and half the lemon coarsely; combine with undrained canned tomatoes and fresh oregano in large casserole dish, season.
5 Add lamb to dish; rub with extra oil, sprinkle with dried oregano. Slice cheese thickly; place around lamb. Cook, covered, in oven, 1¾ hours. Uncover; cook about 30 minutes or until lamb is cooked as desired.
6 Meanwhile, juice remaining lemon; combine juice with yogurt and mint in small bowl. Serve sliced lamb with capsicum sauce, cheese and mint yogurt.

prep + cook time 3 hours
serves 6
nutritional count per serving
40.1g total fat (16.3g saturated fat);
2939kJ (703 cal);
16.4g carbohydrate;
66.7g protein; 3.8g fibre

tip Japanese breadcrumbs are also known as panko breadcrumbs. They are found with packaged breadcrumbs in most supermarkets.

cooking techniques

Washing leeks removes any grit from the inside layers. Cut in half lengthwise, stopping at the root. Fan the layers out and wash under fast-running cold water.

To prepare asparagus, snap the woody end off the asparagus by holding it close to the base and bending it until it snaps. Discard the woody end. Trim asparagus with a vegetable peeler.

To trim beetroot, cut the stems to 2cm (¾-inch) of the bulb, and don't trim the root at the base of the plant. This stops the colour from bleeding during cooking.

To grate beetroot, use the course (large) holes of the grater. It's best to wear disposable gloves as the juice can stain your hands.

When cutting a chilli on the diagonal, leave it whole. The seeds are the heat source, so if you are intolerant of high heat levels, remove the seeds and membranes, or use less chilli.

To grate ginger, peel the piece of ginger with a vegetable peeler or small knife, cutting away awkward knobs and creases. Use the small holes on a box grater, or a rasp grater (thin metal graters), such as a Microplane grater (pictured above), to finely grate the ginger.

To crush garlic, press unpeeled garlic firmly with the side of a large knife (top) crushing the clove. Pull off the papery skin and chop the clove finely with the knife. A garlic press (bottom) removes and leaves the skin behind while crushing the garlic.

To use fresh thyme leaves, hold the top of the stem with one hand and run the fingers of the other hand down the stem to strip off the leaves. Any small, thin stems that break away with the leaves are fine to use.

To chop shallots, cut in half through the root. Make horizontal and vertical cuts in each half, but don't cut all the way through; chop finely.

To crush, grind or blend spices in a mortar and pestle, first place them in the mortar (bowl) then pound them vigorously with the pestle until they are as coarse or as fine as needed.

To slice a capsicum, cut the top and bottom off and stand it on one end; slice down removing all the flesh. Remove and discard the seeds and membranes, and slice the flesh.

Chiffonade is a way of cutting green leaves into long, thin strips. Lay leaves flat on top of each other, then roll up tightly and cut into thin slices.

Pitting an olive is easy with an olive pitter, pictured; just put the olive in the cup and push, and out pops the seed. To do this by hand, crush the olive with the flat side of a large knife and slip the seed out. The olives will then be easy to chop.

To peel a prawn, hold the body with one hand, twist the head with the other and pull it away from the body. Roll the shell, with the legs still attached, from the underside off the body. If removing the tail, squeeze the tail on both sides to release the shell from the flesh and remove.

To cut an onion into wedges, cut the onion in half lengthways through the root. Remove the papery outer skin. Lie the onion cut-side down and cut the onion lengthways through the root into triangular-shaped wedges. The root holds the wedges together.

To cut a cauliflower into florets, remove the leaves, then cut and remove most of the core. Cut off the florets where they join the centre core. Cut into any size you like by simply cutting through the stem and head of each floret. You can also break the florets off the core using your hands.

glossary

ALLSPICE also called pimento or jamaican pepper, tastes like a combination of nutmeg, cumin, clove and cinnamon – all spices. Available in ground form, or as berries, from good spice shops.

ALMONDS flat, pointy-tipped nuts with a pitted brown shell enclosing a creamy white kernel covered by a brown skin.
slivered small pieces cut lengthways.

BACON SLICES also known as bacon rashers, made from cured and smoked side of pork.

BAY LEAF aromatic leaves from the bay tree. Available fresh and dried.

BEANS
cannellini small, dried white bean similar in appearance and flavour to great northern, navy or haricot beans. See also white beans.
green also known as french or string beans (although the tough string they once had has generally been bred out of them), this long thin fresh bean is consumed in its entirety once cooked.
kidney medium-sized red or white bean, slightly floury in texture yet sweet in flavour; sold dried or canned.
sprouts (bean shoots); tender new growths of assorted beans and seeds grown for consumption. The most readily available are mung bean, soya bean, alfalfa and snow pea sprouts.
white in this book, some recipes may simply call for "white beans", a generic term we use for canned or dried cannellini, haricot, navy or great northern beans.

BREADCRUMBS
packaged prepared fine-textured, but crunchy, white breadcrumbs.
japanese also known as panko; has a lighter texture than Western-style breadcrumbs. Sold at Asian grocery stores and some larger supermarkets. Unless you make coarse breadcrumbs from white bread that's either quite stale or gently toasted, nothing is an adequate substitution. Has a crunchy texture and a delicate, golden colour. Use stale breadcrumbs instead, but the texture will be different.

BUTTER use salted or unsalted (sweet) butter; 125g is equal to one stick (4 ounces) of butter.

BUTTERNUT PUMPKIN also known as squash; pear-shaped with golden skin and orange flesh.

CAPERS the grey-green buds of a warm climate (usually Mediterranean) shrub, sold either dried and salted or pickled in a vinegar brine. *Baby capers*, those picked early, are very small, fuller-flavoured and more expensive than the full-size ones. Capers, whether packed in brine or in salt, must be rinsed well before using.

CARDAMOM can be purchased in pod, seed or ground form. Has a distinctive aromatic, sweetly rich flavour.

CHEESE
fetta Greek in origin; a crumbly textured goat's- or sheep-milk cheese having a sharp, salty taste.
goat's made from goat's milk, has an earthy, strong taste; available in soft and firm textures, in various shapes and sizes, sometimes rolled in ash or herbs.
gruyère a hard-rind Swiss cheese with small holes and a nutty, slightly salty flavour. A popular cheese for soufflés.
mozzarella a soft, spun-curd cheese. Has a low melting point and an elastic texture when heated; used to add texture rather than flavour. *Bocconcini* is a walnut-sized, fresh, baby mozzarella. Spoils rapidly, so must be kept under refrigeration, in brine, for one or two days at most.
parmesan also known as parmigiana; a hard, grainy cow's-milk cheese. The curd is salted in brine for a month before being aged for up to two years.
ricotta sweet, moist, white cow's-milk cheese with a slightly grainy texture. The name roughly translates as "cooked again" and refers to ricotta's manufacture from a whey that is itself a by-product of other cheese making.

CHILLI available in many different types and sizes. Use rubber gloves when seeding and chopping fresh chillies as they can burn your skin. Removing seeds and membranes lessens the heat level.
cayenne a thin-fleshed, long, very hot, usually ground, dried red chilli.
korean chilli paste (gochujang, kocchujan) a fermented red chilli and soya bean paste.
long red available both fresh and dried; a generic term used for any long (about 6cm-8cm), thin, moderately hot, chilli.
powder the Asian variety is the hottest, made from dried ground thai chillies. Can be used instead of fresh chillies in the proportion of ½ teaspoon chilli powder to 1 medium chopped fresh red chilli.
thai also known as "scuds"; tiny, very hot and bright red or green in colour.

CHINESE COOKING WINE also known as shao hsing or chinese rice wine; made from fermented rice, wheat, sugar and salt. Found in Asian food shops; if you can't find it, use mirin or sherry, instead.

CHIVES related to the onion and leek; has a subtle onion flavour.

CINNAMON dried inner bark of the shoots of the cinnamon tree; available in stick (quill) or ground form.

COCONUT CREAM obtained from the first pressing of the coconut flesh alone, without the addition of water; the second pressing (less rich) is sold as coconut milk.

CORIANDER also known as pak chee, cilantro or chinese parsley; a bright-green leafy herb with a pungent flavour. Both the stems and roots are used in Thai cooking; wash well before using. Coriander seeds are also available but are no substitute for fresh coriander, as the taste is very different.

CREAM
pouring we use fresh cream, unless otherwise stated; also known as single cream and pure cream. It has no additives unlike commercially thickened cream. Minimum fat content 35%.
sour commercially-cultured soured cream. Minimum fat content 35%.

CURRANTS, DRIED tiny, seedless, almost black raisins. Not the same as fresh currants.

FENNEL also known as finocchio or anise; a roundish, crunchy, pale green-white vegetable. The bulb has a slightly sweet, anise flavour, but the leaves have a much stronger taste. Also sometimes the name given to the dried seeds of the plant, which have a stronger licorice flavour.

FISH FILLETS, FIRM WHITE any boneless firm white fish fillet – bream, blue-eye, swordfish, ling, whiting or sea perch are all fine. Check for any small pieces of bone in the fillets and use tweezers to remove them.

FLOUR
plain an all-purpose wheat flour.
self-raising plain flour sifted with baking powder in the proportion of 1 cup flour to 2 teaspoons baking powder. Also known as self-rising.

GARAM MASALA a blend of spices based on cardamom, cinnamon, cloves, fennel, coriander and cumin, roasted and ground together. Black pepper and chilli can be added for a hotter version.

GINGER, FRESH also known as green or root ginger; the thick gnarled root of a tropical plant.

HORSERADISH CREAM commercially prepared creamy paste made of oil, vinegar, grated horseradish and sugar.

KITCHEN STRING made of a natural product, such as cotton, so it neither affects the flavour of the food it's tied around nor melts when heated.

LEMON GRASS a tall, clumping, lemon-smelling and tasting, sharp-edged aromatic tropical grass; the white lower part of the stem is used, finely chopped.

MAPLE SYRUP, PURE a thin syrup distilled from the sap of the maple tree. Maple-flavoured syrup or pancake syrup is not an adequate substitute for the real thing.

MIRIN a champagne-coloured Japanese cooking wine; made of glutinous rice and alcohol and used expressly for cooking. Should not be confused with sake.

MUSTARD
dijon a pale brown, distinctively flavoured, fairly mild french mustard.
wholegrain also known as seeded mustard. A french-style coarse-grain mustard made from dijon mustard and crushed mustard seeds.

NOODLES
bean thread vermicelli also known as wun sen, cellophane or glass noodles because they are transparent when cooked. Made from mung bean paste. White in colour (not off-white like rice vermicelli), very delicate and fine. Must be soaked to soften before use.
fresh egg also known as ba mee or yellow noodles; made from wheat flour and eggs. Range in size from very fine strands to wide, spaghetti-like pieces as thick as a shoelace. Also sold dried.
hokkien also known as stir-fry noodles; fresh wheat noodles resembling thick, yellow-brown spaghetti needing no pre-cooking before use.
rice vermicelli also known as sen mee, mei fun or bee hoon. Similar to bean thread noodles, only longer and made with rice flour instead of mung bean starch. Before using, soak in hot water until softened, boil briefly then rinse with hot water.
udon available fresh and dried; these broad, white, wheat Japanese noodles are similar to the ones in home-made chicken noodle soup.

OIL
olive made from ripened olives. Extra virgin and virgin are the first and second press, respectively, and are considered the best; the extra light or light name on other types refers to taste, not fat levels.
peanut pressed from ground peanuts; the most commonly used oil in Asian cooking because of its capacity to handle high heat without burning (high smoke point).
vegetable sourced from plants.

ONIONS
green also known as scallion or, incorrectly, shallot; an immature onion picked before the bulb has formed, has a long, bright-green edible stalk.

red also known as spanish, red spanish or bermuda onion; a sweet-flavoured, large, purple-red onion.
shallots also called french shallots, golden shallots or eschalots; small, brown-skinned, elongated members of the onion family. Grows in tight clusters similar to garlic.
spring have small white bulbs and long, narrow green-leafed tops.

PAPRIKA ground dried sweet red capsicum (bell pepper); there are many types available, including sweet, hot, mild and smoked.

PARSLEY, FLAT-LEAF also known as continental or italian parsley.

PASTA
penne translated literally as "quills"; a ridged pasta cut into short lengths on the diagonal. Great with chunky sauces.
shells shell-shaped pasta ranging from tiny to very large in size.

PASTES
harissa a very hot Moroccan sauce or paste made from dried chillies, cumin, garlic, oil and caraway seeds; there are many different brands available on the market, and the strengths vary enormously. If you have a low heat-level tolerance, you may find harissa, too hot to tolerate. It is available in supermarkets and Middle-Eastern grocery stores.
red curry a very popular curry paste; is a medium-hot blend of chilli, garlic, onion, lemon grass, spice, galangal and salt.

PINE NUTS also known as pignoli; not, in fact, a nut but a small, cream-coloured kernel from pine cones.

PISTACHIO pale green, delicately flavoured nut inside hard off-white shells. To peel, soak shelled nuts in boiling water for about 5 minutes; drain, then pat dry with absorbent paper. Rub skins with a cloth to peel.

PITTA BREAD also known as lebanese bread; a wheat-flour pocket bread sold in large flat pieces that separate into two thin rounds. Also available in small thick pieces called pocket pitta.

POLENTA also known as cornmeal; a flour-like cereal made of dried corn (maize) sold ground in different textures; also the name of the dish made from it.

PORK BELLY a lower-cost cut of meat due to the relatively high traces of fat in it. However, this means that the cuts are ideal for longer cooking periods and recipes where the meat might dry out.

POTATO
baby new also known as chats; not a separate variety but an early harvest with very thin skin; good unpeeled.
kipfler small, finger-shaped potato having a nutty flavour.

PRESERVED LEMON RIND a North African specialty; lemons are quartered and preserved in salt and lemon juice. To use, remove and discard pulp, squeeze juice from rind, rinse rind well then slice thinly.

QUAIL EGGS are available from some specialist butchers, chicken shops and delicatessens. The highly speckled shells range in colour from dark brown to blue or white.

RAS EL HANOUT is a classic spice blend used in Moroccan cooking. Meaning "top of the shop", this is the very best spice blend that a spice merchant has to offer.

RED BEAN PASTE made from adzuki (azuki) beans; small dark red, oval beans with a beige ridge along one side. The dried been is processed and used in many Asian recipes including as a highly sweetened bean paste that is used in sweet soups and desserts. Available from Asian food stores.

RICE
arborio small, round-grain rice, well-suited to absorb a large amount of liquid; especially suitable for risottos.
basmati a fragrant, white, long-grained rice that is most usually associated with the food of India. Wash several times before cooking.
long-grain an elongated grain that remains separate when cooked; the most popular steaming rice in Asia.

ROCKET also known as arugula, rugula and rucola; a peppery-tasting green leaf that can be used similarly to baby spinach leaves, eaten raw in salad or used in cooking. *Baby rocket leaves*, also known as wild rocket, are both smaller and less peppery.

SAFFRON THREADS available in strands or ground form; imparts a yellow-orange colour to food once infused. Store in the freezer.

SAKE Japan's favourite alcoholic drink; rice wine that is also used in cooking, marinating and as part of dipping sauces. If unavailable, dry sherry, vermouth or brandy can be used as a substitute.

SAUCES
char siu a Chinese barbecue sauce made from sugar, water, salt, honey, fermented soya bean paste, soy sauce, malt syrup and spices. It can be found at most supermarkets.
fish also known as nam pla or nuoc nam; made from pulverised salted fermented fish (most often anchovies). Has a pungent smell and strong taste. There are many versions of varying intensity available, so use according to your taste.
soy made from fermented soya beans. Several variations are available in most supermarkets and Asian food stores.
japanese soy all-purpose low-sodium soy sauce made with more wheat content than its Chinese counterparts. Possibly the best table soy and the one to choose if you only want one variety.
light soy a pale, fairly thin, but salty tasting, sauce; used in dishes in which the natural colour of the ingredients is to be maintained. Don't confuse with salt-reduced or low-sodium soy sauces.
tomato also known as ketchup or catsup; made from tomatoes, vinegar and spices.
tomato pasta made of a blend of tomatoes, herbs and spices.
worcestershire a dark-coloured sauce made from garlic, soy sauce, tamarind, onions, molasses, lime, anchovies, vinegar and seasonings.

SHALLOTS, see onions.

SPINACH also known as english spinach and, incorrectly, silver beet. Its thick, soft oval leaves and green stems are both edible. Baby spinach is also available.

SUGAR
brown an extremely soft, finely granulated sugar retaining molasses for its characteristic colour and flavour.
caster also known as superfine or finely granulated table sugar.
palm also known as nam tan pip, jawa, jaggery or gula melaka; made from the sap of the sugar palm tree. Light brown to black in colour and usually sold in rock-hard cakes. Substitute with brown sugar, if unavailable.
white a coarsely granulated table sugar, also known as crystal sugar.

TABASCO brand name of a very fiery sauce made from vinegar, hot red chillies and salt.

VEAL
osso buco literally meaning "bone with a hole", osso buco is cut from the shin of the hind leg. It is also known as knuckle.
schnitzel thinly sliced steak available crumbed or plain (uncrumbed); we use plain schnitzel, sometimes called escalopes, in our recipes.

VINEGAR
balsamic made from the juice of Trebbiano grapes; is a deep rich brown colour with a sweet and sour flavour. There are now many balsamic vinegars on the market ranging in pungency and quality depending on how long they have been aged. Quality can be determined up to a point by price; use the most expensive sparingly.
red wine based on fermented red wine.
white wine made from white wine.

WOMBOK also known as chinese cabbage, peking or napa cabbage; elongated in shape with pale green, crinkly leaves, this is the most common cabbage in South-East Asia.

ZUCCHINI also known as courgette; a small, pale- or dark-green, yellow or white vegetable belonging to the squash family.

index

Published in 2012 by ACP Books, Sydney
ACP Books are published by ACP Magazines Limited,
a division of Nine Entertainment Co.

ACP BOOKS
General manager Christine Whiston
Editor-in-chief Susan Tomnay
Creative director & designer Hieu Chi Nguyen
Art director Hannah Blackmore
Senior editor Wendy Bryant
Food director Pamela Clark
Food editor Rebecca Squadrito
Sales & rights director Brian Cearnes
Special sales manager Simone Aquilina
Acting marketing manager Sonia Scali
Marketing assistant Madeleine Jelfs
Senior business analyst Rebecca Varela
Operations manager David Scotto
Production manager Victoria Jefferys
Circulation manager Sarah Lloyd
Circulation analyst Nicole Pearson
Published by ACP Books, a division of
ACP Magazines Ltd, 54 Park St, Sydney;
GPO Box 4088, Sydney, NSW 2001.
phone (02) 9282 8618; fax (02) 9267 9438.

acpbooks@acpmagazines.com.au;
www.acpbooks.com.au

Printed by Toppan Printing Co, China.

Australia Distributed by Network Services,
phone +61 2 9282 8777; fax +61 2 9264 3278;
networkweb@networkservicescompany.com.au
New Zealand Distributed by Netlink Distribution Company,
phone (64 9) 366 9966; ask@ndc.co.nz
South Africa Distributed by PSD Promotions,
phone (27 11) 392 6065/6/7; fax (27 11) 392 6079/80;
orders@psdprom.co.za

Title: One-dish dinners / Food director, Pamela Clark.
ISBN: 9781 74245 235 7 (pbk.)
Notes: Includes index.
Subjects: One-dish meals.
Other Authors/Contributors: Clark, Pamela.
Also Titled: Australian women's weekly.
Dewey Number: 641.82

© ACP Magazines Ltd 2012
ABN 18 053 273 546
This publication is copyright. No part of it may be
reproduced or transmitted in any form without the
written permission of the publishers.

Recipe development Lara Reynolds, Jane Collings,
Alexandra Somerville
Nutritional information Rebecca Squadrito

Photographer Louise Lister
Stylist Jane Hann
Food preparation Lara Reynolds
Cover italian-style lamb cutlets, page 14

To order books
phone 136 116 (within Australia) or
order online at www.acpbooks.com.au
Send recipe enquiries to:
recipeenquiries@acpmagazines.com.au

First published in 2012

ACP Books are published by ACP Magazines Limited,

a division of Nine Entertainment Co.

54 Park St, Sydney

GPO Box 4088, Sydney, NSW 2001.

phone (02) 9282 8618; fax (02) 9267 9438

acpbooks@acpmagazines.com.au; www.acpbooks.com.au

ACP BOOKS

General Manager - Christine Whiston

Editor-in-Chief - Susan Tomnay

Creative Director - Hieu Chi Nguyen

Food Director - Pamela Clark

Published and Distributed in the United Kingdom by Octopus Publishing Group

Endeavour House

189 Shaftesbury Avenue

London WC2H 8JY

United Kingdom

phone (+44)(0)207 632 5400; fax (+44)(0)207 632 5405

info@octopus-publishing.co.uk;

www.octopusbooks.co.uk

Printed by Toppan Printing Co., China

International foreign language rights, Brian Cearnes, ACP Books bcearnes@acpmagazines.com.au

A catalogue record for this book is available from the British Library.

ISBN 978-1-907428-48-7

© ACP Magazines Ltd 2012

ABN 18 053 273 546